BREAKING THE UNWRITTEN

*How One Girl's Courage Sparked a
Revolution in African Women's Health*

BLANDINE UMUZIRANENGE

STARDOM BOOKS

www.StardomBooks.com

STARDOM BOOKS
112 Bordeaux Ct.
Coppell, TX 75019, USA

Copyright © 2026 by Blandine Umuziranenge

All rights reserved. No part of this book may be reproduced or used
in any manner without the written permission of the copyright owner,
except for the use of quotations in a book review.

FIRST EDITION MAY 2026

STARDOM BOOKS, LLC.

112 Bordeaux Ct. Coppell, TX 75019, USA

www.stardombooks.com

Stardom Books

United States and India

The author and publishers have made all reasonable efforts to contact copyright holders for permission and apologize for any omissions or errors in the form of credits given. Corrections may be made to future editions.

BREAKING THE UNWRITTEN

How One Girl's Courage Sparked a Revolution in African Women's Health

BLANDINE UMUZIRANENGE

P. 182

cm. 13.97 X 21.59

Category : BIO026000 — Biography & Autobiography / Personal Memoirs

BIO051000 — Biography & Autobiography / Women

SEL021000 — Self-Help / Personal Growth / General

ISBN : 978-1-957456-96-6

Dedication

To the young girl who feels unheard, who carries the weight of doubt, and who navigates her path without a hand to hold, may you find your voice within these pages.

To the entrepreneur standing in the difficult middle of their journey, weary but still reaching for the change they aspire to bring to this world, this is your map through the unknown.

And to the rare souls who choose to help not out of duty, but out of a genuine will to see others rise, you are the seeds of my impact today and the forest yet to grow.

I dedicate this book to you.

Acknowledgments

Writing this book has been both a professional and personal journey, and I am deeply grateful to all who made it possible.

First, I extend my sincere thanks to everyone who lifted me up each time this journey felt harder. To those who reminded me that I was born to create impact, not to give up every time I felt discouraged: your belief in me was the fuel I needed to keep moving forward.

I am also indebted to the programs, mentors, and coaches throughout my journey who sharpened my brain with insights, tools, and strategies. You made the impossible sound possible, and together we turned those visions into a reality for everyone to witness.

To my family and friends, your unwavering support has been my anchor. My family, in particular, shaped the human I am today; you taught me to live by principles and serve by values. You are the foundation of my character and the heart of my mission.

I would like to thank Stardom Books and every member of the team who worked on this project. Your patience and care in turning my story into this piece of art have been invaluable. I am also grateful to those who believed in me even when I struggled to believe in myself, and to everyone who joined me on this journey of changemaking, whether you were there before it had a name or have joined us now that it has made a meaningful impact. You are the reason the rope of my impact never broke.

To those who opened doors and invited me into rooms I never dreamed of entering: thank you for helping me imagine the impossible. And finally, to every partner who trusted me with funding or a recommendation to support our mission at Kosmotive: I carry your trust as my currency. This book is a testament to our collective effort to build a world of dignity and health equity.

Contents

Introduction

There are many stories told about courage. Most of them are loud. They begin with triumph, with moments that demand attention, with victories that can be named and applauded. This is not one of those stories. This story begins much earlier. Before confidence had language. Before strength knew its own name. It begins in small rooms, in quiet corners, in moments that did not look important at the time. It begins in the space between wanting and daring. In the silence where questions first formed but were not yet spoken. In the lives of people who learned early that the world does not always make room for those who dream differently.

If you are looking for a story that tells you how to be brave, this book may disappoint you. It does not offer instructions. It does not promise certainty. It does not pretend that courage arrives neatly or stays once it comes. What it offers instead is something more honest. A voice that has walked through uncertainty and kept moving anyway. A companion for the parts of your journey that do not feel heroic yet. I did not write this book because I had all the answers. I wrote it because I learned what it means to keep going without clarity, without permission, and without the comfort of seeing someone like myself succeed before me.

I wrote it because I know what it feels like to stand at the edge of something unnamed and wonder whether stepping forward is worth the cost.

This book exists not to impress, not to instruct, and not to offer a polished version of resilience. It exists to witness. To sit beside the reader rather than stand ahead of them. To say, quietly and without performance, that uncertainty does not mean you are weak, and fear does not mean you are failing. Often, they mean you are beginning. If you are reading this, there is a chance you already recognize yourself here.

This book is for the girl who knows she is meant for more, even if she cannot yet explain what that more looks like. For the one who feels out of place, not because she lacks ability, but because the path laid out before her does not fit the shape of her questions. It is for the first in her family, her village, her community, her world. For the one who has been told, directly or indirectly, that certain things are not meant for people like her. It is also for the dreamer who started something and then stopped. Not because they lacked discipline, but because doubt arrived early and support did not. For the entrepreneur who looked around and saw others moving faster, backed by networks, resources, and confidence that seemed inherited rather than earned. For anyone who has ever thought, maybe I cannot do this because no one like me ever has.

If that thought has ever lived inside you, this book is for you. You will not find strategies or step-by-step formulas here. You will not be given a checklist for success. What you will find instead is something more difficult to quantify but far more enduring. You will find presence. You will find recognition. You will find a voice that understands the weight of invisible rules and the quiet exhaustion of trying to grow in spaces that were not designed for you. I did not begin this journey with confidence. I began with trembling hands and a heart that felt louder than my courage. I began with questions I was afraid to ask out loud. With instincts I did not yet trust. With a sense that something in me was restless, even when I could not name what it wanted. Step by step, often without realizing it, I learned to listen to that restlessness instead of silencing it.

That is what this book is really about. It is about small beginnings that do not announce themselves. About defiance that looks like persistence rather than rebellion. About the kind of power that grows slowly, quietly, and without witnesses. It is about learning to stand without certainty, to move without applause, and to keep faith with yourself when the world has not yet decided what to make of you.

There are moments in life when courage feels dramatic. This book is not interested in those moments alone. It is interested in the days that came before them. The days when no one was watching. The days when doubt felt logical. The days when giving up would have made sense. It is interested in the invisible labor of becoming. The emotional negotiations, the private resilience, the decisions made in silence that later shape everything. I have learned that bravery is not always the act of pushing forward. Sometimes it is the act of staying. Staying curious when answers are scarce. Staying kind when bitterness would be easier. Staying connected to a sense of possibility when evidence is thin. For this generation, whether young in age or simply young in spirit, bravery is less about fearlessness and more about steadiness. The ability to remain resilient, composed, and hopeful in the face of uncertainty.

Hope, in this book, is not a naive optimism. It is not the denial of difficulty. It is the decision to keep believing that your story is not finished, even when the middle chapters feel heavy.

It is the refusal to let circumstance be the final author of your life. As you move through these pages, you will encounter fear in many forms. Fear of failing. Fear of being seen. Fear of being the first. Fear of being misunderstood. Fear of success that arrives before you feel ready to carry it. This book does not promise to remove those fears. Instead, it asks a different question. What if fear is not the enemy, but the signal? What if it appears not to stop you, but to tell you that something meaningful is at stake?

You will also encounter humor here, not as decoration, but as survival. Laughter, in these pages, is not about making light of pain. It is about reclaiming agency. About refusing to let difficulty harden you. About remembering that even in serious journeys, humanity matters. There will be moments of vulnerability. Not the kind that seeks sympathy, but the kind that builds trust. There will be truths shared without polish, because the goal of this book is not perfection, but connection. I have included the parts of the journey that felt uncertain, awkward, and unfinished, because those are often the parts readers recognize most clearly in themselves.

This is not a story about arriving. It is a story about becoming. You do not need to read this book quickly. You do not need to agree with everything in it. You do not need to see yourself on every page. Take what resonates. Leave what does not. Let the words sit with you rather than rush you. This is not a book that demands transformation. It invites reflection. If, two years from now, even one person reads this and feels less alone in their hesitation, less ashamed of their doubt, or more willing to take a first step simply because they have seen someone else walk without a map, then this book has already done its work.

If it helps someone begin, or helps someone continue when quitting feels easier, then its purpose is fulfilled.

I believe deeply that systems change when stories change. That visibility matters. That seeing possibility where there was none before can quietly shift what people believe is allowed. I may not yet know all the ways this book will travel, or who it will reach, but I know why it exists. It exists to remind you that you are not strange for wanting more. That your questions are not inconveniences. That your pace does not invalidate your direction. Most of all, it exists to offer companionship. So, if you are standing at the edge of your own beginning, uncertain, curious, and quietly hopeful, come with me.

We will walk this part together.

CHAPTER 1

When the Path Isn't Paved for You

*'B**landine, the girl who hid books under her skirt.'* That's probably how the students and teachers in my school still remember me. I was quite a handful as a child, a little too curious and bold for the adults' taste. A raging headache to both my teachers and parents, making beatings and scoldings an integral part of my childhood.

In my sixth class, I had a math teacher who was extremely strict and beat kids for even the smallest mistake. For every wrong answer, he would add one beating to our tally and give us all of the punishment together. By the time it's Friday, most of us will have a good number of beats ready to be received. With my notorious energy and curiosity, I would have collected around 50 to 60 beatings every week. There was no way that I would survive that many beatings, nor did I plan to, so I decided to play smart by wearing two uniform dresses under my current one, and even hid a couple of books inside my dress to fool the teacher. My plan was successful for a while, and things were going really smoothly for me.

But to my bad luck, on this particular Friday, when I was all prepared to receive punishment with my hidden books and two sets of uniforms, the math teacher had to leave the classroom for an emergency. Upon his instruction, another teacher came in to hand out punishment, who had a habit of grabbing the uniform dress in one hand before beating us.

So, when he grabbed my uniform, he could feel that the dress was unusually thick. When he tried to hit, it was like hitting a drum. Of course, as a teacher who has seen countless students trying to outsmart them over the years, he immediately caught on to what was happening. He asked me to take out the books, and took the second dress I was layering, tied it around my neck, and dragged me to the corridor where the p3 and p4 classes were. He made me stand in the corridor the entire day as punishment. He expected me to feel sorry and scared, but instead, I was just smiling and waving at the kids in the class. All of them looked out of the window to see what was going on, and kids started retelling this story from class to class, and soon it became a school legend.

People still laugh about this incident. At that time, it may have looked like just another stubborn act from a difficult child. But it didn't come from nowhere. That instinct to resist, to improvise, to outsmart rules instead of quietly submitting to them, had been forming long before I ever sat in a classroom. It was shaped by the place I grew up, the lives I watched unfold around me, and the narrow paths I was told were the only ones available to me.

The Environment That Raised Me

During my childhood, I had briefly stayed over in refugee camps due to political instabilities in the country. I still vividly remember those days. Rows and rows of tents, big families with a bunch of children huddling together in a small place, and fathers leaving in the morning in search of a job that will feed their families. The mothers are sweating in the kitchen, cooking for everyone, and instructing their daughters on the art of homemaking, while the boys run around here and there. My family was just one among the hundreds.

That environment shaped how I saw the world long before I understood it.

Me and my mother and siblings at the refugee camp

My father used to leave every morning for work, and my mother, who had worked at a bank, would go to a nearby orphanage to help out. During that time, I was the youngest of my siblings, and I had a four-year age gap with my elder siblings, who would all go to school. So, most of the time, I play by myself, trying to figure out how to entertain myself. I recall my parents being worried about me because of this. I really was quite a handful as a child, and the loneliness did not help at all. This continued even after returning from the refugee camp. If I get bored, I often leave home and gallivant around the neighborhood without informing my parents or even asking for permission. I loved hearing people's stories, so I would walk up to random people and engage them in conversation, then go back home to tell my mom all the stories I'd heard.

However, the world I was exploring was not a safe one. There were many landmines near our home. Most of the stories included people accidentally stepping on a mine and getting injured and losing limbs. This used to drive my parents insane, thinking that I had witnessed all these dangerous things firsthand.

They used to scold me, saying I shouldn't leave the house or go talk with strangers.

But, when I ask them why, none of them ever bothers to give me an explanation. So, I would go on my adventures the next day because, in my head, I was not doing anything wrong, and my parents would keep scolding me without ever explaining why. As a child, I couldn't understand why they were hitting me, but as an adult, I could understand why my parents were worried. But at that age, a child just needed entertainment and not to be bored. I still remember standing near the gate waiting for the people who went to market and following them as they told stories. I think my parents thought, "She is mad, because she follows everyone as long as they have stories."

But for me, it was never about being strange. It was about trying to understand a world that no one was explaining to me. I was just a child who kept asking "why" in a world built on "because we said so." And that wasn't just in my home. It was everywhere around me.

Walking down a different and new path was something my society and community could never comprehend. And every family and every parent lived in fear of what society thought, and took its words as law. "No one in your family or community has ever done that." The amount of time I had heard this line growing up is outrageous. You can't become something if no one in your family or community has done that. If you are thinking about doing something new, everyone will speak against it.

They believed that if no one has ever done something, you will definitely fail if you try to do it. Unless, of course, you are born with a silver spoon and can afford to fail and try again. But for people in my village, walking on a new path was a guarantee for failure, and something they looked down upon.

That was the logic I grew up around: safety in sameness, and fear of anything different. And this fear of stepping outside the familiar did not fall equally on everyone. It had a shape. It had a hierarchy. And very early on, I learned that it had a gender.

The Weight of What Was Expected of Me

The pressure to stay within the known path was most evident in the expectations placed on girls. I grew up in a very conservative and patriarchal society where girls were expected to fill certain roles, and household chores were one of them. My mother would constantly nag my sisters and me about cleaning, cooking, washing plates, and this and that. I don't know whether my sisters truly loved doing these things or were simply pretending to, so our mother wouldn't nag us, but I was never a fan of household chores. If there was a way I could get away with not doing any of it, I would have done that without a second's notice.

But what frustrated me even more than the chores themselves were the questions that followed if we didn't seem to enjoy them: "Which man will choose you if you can't cook? Which man will marry you if you can't clean?" It was as if our existence and our worth were decided by how useful or desirable we were to men. That idea frustrated me deeply and made me even more rebellious. I wanted to be someone of value on my own merit, not because of whether a man found me desirable.

This way of thinking didn't just show up in small comments; it shaped how girls were raised to think about their entire future. It felt like fear was being planted early, the fear of becoming a "bad" woman, the fear of having a past that society could whisper about. I have never seen a man's past being questioned at the time of marriage, only a woman's.

That fear of being judged, of being talked about, quietly ruled the lives of the young girls around me.

Living under those expectations did not make me quieter or more careful. It did the opposite. The more narrowly my future was described to me, the more urgently I wanted to step outside of it, even if I did not yet have the words for what I was running toward. I only knew that staying still, staying inside, staying obedient felt like its own kind of disappearance.

And that is why I began to look for spaces where I could be more than just a girl. That was why school felt like an opening to me. It was a door out of boredom, out of silence, out of a life already being quietly decided on my behalf. It did not feel like an obligation. It felt like the first place where I might be allowed to become something different.

The Moment I First Questioned the Script

The age at which you could start school was seven, but I was not patient enough to wait until then. From the age of four, I used to pester my siblings and parents by asking to go to school. They would always say, wait till I was seven. The rest of my siblings were already in school. I remember asking one of my sisters, who had learned to count, how long I had to wait. I was really eager to go to school, and more than that, I couldn't stand having to stay at home. So, whenever my siblings left for school in the morning, I would also leave home for my daily adventures. By the time they came back, I would return home too, after spending the entire day outside. I would meet kids on their way to school and ask them all sorts of questions about what they were studying, and I would also go door-to-door to meet the women who lived there and talk with them. This became my routine.

Every time I came back, I would go straight to my mother and tell her everything I had learned that day; the children I had met, what they were studying in P1 and P2, and also the stories about who was expecting a baby and who had just given birth. By the end of the month, my mother had had enough of my wandering and talking and agreed to send me to school the following year.

But something else stayed with me from those days.

During these adventures, I grew close to the women who stayed home. Every time I passed their tent, I would speak with them. I remember how sometimes they told me they were going to give birth, and then they would return from the hospital with no baby. Even at that young age, I wanted to stop such things from happening. I thought I could do that by becoming a doctor.

I think this was my first ambition, or aim. It was the first time I connected what I was seeing to something I could become. Many kids say they want to be an astronaut or a pilot, but that usually comes after they start school. For me, this came much earlier.

A Series of Small Rebellions

If I look back, my life did not change because of one big decision. It changed because of a series of small rebellions. Moments where I chose not to follow something that did not make sense to me.

One of the first times this had real consequences was with the scholarship.

The scholarship story

In our place, once you graduate from high school and have good scores, the government often offers scholarships to certain universities.

I also received a scholarship to the University of Education. But at the time, I wasn't sure about what it was that I wanted from my life. However, the one thing I knew was that I didn't want to become a teacher. I knew in my heart that I couldn't teach. My interest leaned more towards technology, and I expressed my desire not to take the scholarship in front of my family. It was like I dropped a bomb in the middle of our house. Everyone in the family, the neighbors, and the community started shouting at me and lecturing me, saying I was making a mistake. No one in our province had ever turned down a scholarship. If you don't have a scholarship, you will have to pay out of pocket, and my father was stern about the fact that he won't spend a single penny on my education if I turn down the scholarship, and that I will be on my own. It was a huge fight. I still had a couple of months to change universities, so I decided to visit the university I wanted and make my case to them. To see whether I can still get the scholarship even if I change my area of study. My father was like, "I won't give you ticket money to go after something that won't work." Then I told them that I would go on foot. After hearing this, my parents said that I can't leave home. That they don't know where I am going, and they don't trust me enough.

At that time, it was my sister who supported me. She said that if I can no longer stay in my parents' home, I am free to stay at her place. "At least you will be allowed to live your life here," she said in the end. It was a huge relief to me to know that I wasn't alone.

What kept me going were the promises made by the university's principal that I wanted to attend. Since I am asking to be transferred from a highly ranked university to theirs, they said it will be no difficulty for me to get a seat either through internal adjustments or by finding someone to swap seats with me.

This promise drove me forward until I achieved what I set out to do. But this way of thinking had shown up much earlier.

When I was in primary four, I was very small and much younger than other kids because I had started school early. Because of this, I never really fit in the class. The other students were two years older than me and appeared too mature. I didn't even have friends or people to play with. I often used to go to P2, where kids my age were, and play with them.

That year, there was a sudden surge in popularity for a chewing gum brand featuring stickers of sports players. It was a really big deal. People would pay to collect these stickers. But for me, I didn't have any money to buy stickers or chewing gum. Instead, I paid them using the pages of my notebook. If it were a small player or team, it was one page, but if it were a big team, I had to pay two or three pages.

My parents were not aware that I had used up all my notebooks like this. I only had one book left with a few pages, which I used for all of my subjects. But soon the teacher caught me and reported it to my parents. They decided to make me repeat the class, despite my good scores. When the new year started, my mother told me that I had to sit in P4 again.

But I was not willing to repeat the year. So, I went to P5. I kept my mouth shut and behaved well so no one would know I wasn't supposed to be in the class. However, by the end of the first term, my mother caught on. Since almost a term had passed, they couldn't take me back, and my P5 class teacher also spoke up, saying I was doing well with my studies. I really couldn't imagine going back to the same class and having to sit with new students, and making new friends.

I think that was around the time I started to take my studies and my class really seriously. I was even placed first in my class. That was how much I didn't want to mess up.

I think if I had repeated that class, I would have lost all my motivation and never reached here.

One stubborn streak I had since a young age was that if I didn't understand why, I wouldn't do it, and I think that's why I refused to repeat the class. And this wasn't something that showed up only in school. It followed me everywhere. At home, this made me feel like an oddball, because all of my siblings behaved.

They would stay home the whole day and follow all the written and unwritten rules without ever questioning them. I could never understand the reasons for their obedience. As a child, I genuinely tried to follow my siblings' example, but it didn't work. It only made me restless, and I even ended up making a hole in our fence so I could go out of my house. Sometimes I wonder, "Am I not normal? Am I weird? Because everyone is staying here, they don't have any issues."

There was this one incident with a piercing in my childhood. So, we were not allowed to pierce our ears for religious reasons. And I thought it was weird and didn't make any sense. So, this one time, I took a pin and pierced my own ear. The funny thing was, I didn't do it because I wanted to wear earrings. I didn't even have any earrings. I just did it because I felt like the excuse didn't make sense.

The next morning, my parents saw the piercing, but they didn't believe that it was me who did it. They kept on asking whether someone forcibly pierced it for me. I kept on saying it was I who did it, but they thought I was lying, saying that I couldn't pierce both ears myself without even crying. I got frustrated thinking, "Why can't people trust that I did it?"

Moments like this made me realize that many rules were followed simply because they existed, not because they were understood.

And these rules didn't stop with small things like ear piercing. It showed up in bigger questions, too, especially when it came to religion.

My parents followed different religions and went to different churches. Instead of choosing between the two, I ended up going to a completely different church that was closer to my home. At that time, distance mattered more to me than doctrine. It was simply easier to reach, and that made sense to me. I joined the choir there as a drummer, and over time, it became something I really enjoyed. My mother was happy about this because it kept me occupied and gave her some peace of mind about where I was spending my time. My father, however, had no idea that I was going to a completely different church.

For two years, this continued without any problem. Then came Christmas.

That year, on Christmas morning, my father drove us to church and dropped me off at my mother's church with her. After church, we all came back home to celebrate the evening with family and friends. After the celebration, my parents went to drop off the visitors, and on their way back, they met one of my neighbors who attends my church. He casually mentioned that the band had not sounded as good without me playing the drums. That was the moment my father found out that I had been attending an entirely different church. To say he was shocked would be an understatement. When they returned home, it led to a heated argument. My father demanded that I choose either his church or my mother's. I hadn't meant to make any kind of statement, but now I had to make a decision. So, I chose my mother's church for the same reason I had chosen the first one. It was closer to home. His church was much farther away, and distance still mattered to me more than anything else. But that choice displeased my father even more.

It was confusing to me why, like my parents, I couldn't choose a church on my own. I think I did that a lot in childhood, asking "Why?" for every rule thrust upon me. I kept questioning the unwritten rules that everybody else seemed to follow without hesitation. When the elders said, "Don't leave," no one left. When they said to sleep at this time, everyone slept. Whatever was said, the other children followed without questioning. But I could never do that.

And because of that, there were times when people even started to think that something was wrong with me, that I was possessed, simply because I kept asking why.

Not every rule I questioned led to conflicts as severe as those around religion. Many times, it showed up in smaller ways. In our culture, and perhaps in many others, women were not allowed to whistle. The elders used to say that if a girl whistled at night, she would bring snakes into the house. Like many other rules I had heard growing up, this one also did not make much sense to me, and as expected, I did not follow it.

One evening, around 8 p.m., I was whistling without realizing that my parents were at home. Suddenly, my father came rushing into the room, demanding to know who was making the sound. I panicked and immediately pretended to be asleep, even snoring loudly to make it convincing. At the time, we had only one boy at home, and the blame quickly fell on him. He got slapped by my father, and no one even suspected me for a second. They believed I was someone who could fall asleep very quickly. However, that small lie came with its own consequences. From that day onward, I had to keep up the act of falling asleep quickly every night, even on days when I stayed awake for hours.

Once I went to bed, I could not talk, move around, or make any sound, because I had to maintain the image of being a heavy sleeper so that no one would ever suspect that I had been the one whistling.

For me, hope was never something grand or dramatic. It was simply the idea of being in a place where there were not too many rules, or at least where I could see people doing what they wanted without fear. It meant being somewhere where questions were allowed, or being around people who tried to understand rather than punish.

That kind of hope felt like a luxury I did not grow up with. For many years, fear shaped the way I expressed myself. Even when I had something to say, I would lower my voice first, almost testing whether it was safe to speak. I would watch people's reactions carefully, trying to sense whether I would be beaten or scolded for saying what I thought.

Looking back, I realize that what I was searching for all those years was not freedom in a large sense, but simply understanding. I was looking for a place where questioning was not treated as rebellion, and where being different did not feel like something to be ashamed of.

Environmental Shift: When the World Changed

My high school was a catholic boarding school run by nuns. It was a different experience for me, and I learned and unlearned a lot of things during that period. Till then, I always felt so different from the people around me, and even thought I was a really weird person. But after closely mingling with people around my age in a very different setting, I started to see myself as normal. I could think and wonder without feeling weird or fearing punishment.

My high school student ID card

Me performing comedy alongside a classmate

I changed a lot in this time period. Humor became a part of my character. And I was really doing well in classes. Initially, the mistresses noticed me because I was really small compared to the other students and kept an eye on me. However, once I started getting good grades, teachers started to view me differently.

Me in school uniform

There was a time when the president came to our school to inaugurate a computer lab, and I was chosen to hand the president flowers. This really boosted my self-esteem. It may seem like a very small thing to people outside, or even to you as you are reading this. But it was not the case for me.

To a child who grew up in a refugee camp and was always told you were a little bit weird, this was a huge milestone. It was also a huge deal to me that the headmistress trusted me with this task. I felt like I needed to protect that trust. Even as a child, I was very determined not to mess up that task of handing flowers.

To my Young Readers

Looking back at my younger self, who felt so alone in her world, I wish someone had told me I wasn't weird or that being a girl doesn't have to limit my thinking or dreaming. Looking back, I realize how drastically different my brothers' and my life were. It feels like we had different parents and lived in two different worlds.

No one told my brother that he couldn't climb the tree or wander. I didn't want to limit myself just because I'm a girl. If I'm not doing the same as every other girl, or every other person my age, in my community, or in my family, it doesn't mean that I am weird or crazy.

If you think that you are weird or alone, and unlike other people around you, don't worry, you are not alone. It's okay if you can't see another person who looks like you or thinks like you, or who is exactly like you. Just listen to the voice that is pushing you to do something, as long as you're not harming anyone else. Stick to that. Believe in yourself. And keep looking for others like you, because there are others, trust me. It really gives you strength when you can tap into a community that understands what you're going through. There is a lot of wisdom from people who've gone through the same thing, and an easy way to solve something if you're feeling it's hard.

As someone who had to fight many battles alone, I want every one of you reading this book not to have to go through the same struggles.

If you want to walk on a different path, then walk. Try different things, no matter what people around you say, and do not give up. If others do not believe in your "why" or in what you want to do, that does not mean your way is wrong. It may simply mean that they do not yet understand your vision, or that they only come to believe through actions rather than words.

Do not take their doubts personally, even though it can feel discouraging at times.

The more you continue moving forward and begin to show results, the more those who once discouraged you will slowly begin to stand beside you. That is what happened to me. Over time, I could see that many people wanted to support me, even when I no longer needed as much support as I once did.

What I truly wish is that every girl receives support much earlier in her journey, whether she is still shaping an idea, learning new skills, or taking her first uncertain steps forward. Support should not come only after success, because by that stage, most people have already built their own ways of protecting themselves.

The time people need their closest friends, family, and community the most is not when they succeed, but when they first choose to begin their journey.

Chapter 2

Invisible Rules, Visible Fears

There are rules you grow up knowing because someone sits you down and explains them. And then there are rules that seep into you quietly, without introduction, without explanation, without permission. No one ever announces them. No one ever writes them down. Yet somehow, everyone seems to know them. Everyone follows them. And when you do not, the consequences arrive swiftly, even if you never knew you were breaking anything at all. For a long time, I believed my confusion meant something was wrong with me. I believed that if I felt uncomfortable, uncertain, or restless, it was because I was failing to understand something obvious that everyone else seemed to grasp effortlessly. Only much later did I understand that my discomfort was not a flaw. It was a response. A response to a system that depended on silence more than sense, obedience more than understanding, and conformity more than truth.

I grew up learning, very early, that questioning existing structures was not encouraged. If something was done a certain way, you were expected to do it exactly the same way. Why it was done like that did not matter. Who decided it did not matter. How it came to be did not matter. The rule existed, and that was reason enough. There was an unspoken agreement between adults and children, between authority and obedience. You follow first. You ask later, if ever. And if you did ask, you had to be prepared for the subtle shift in how you were seen. Asking why was rarely treated as curiosity. It was often interpreted as defiance.

This was not something anyone taught me in words. It was something I absorbed through reactions. Through silences that stretched too long. Through looks that lingered a second more than necessary. Through conversations that ended abruptly when my questions entered the room. I quickly learned that certain questions made people uncomfortable, and that discomfort was something you were expected to avoid. The rules were never introduced as rules. They arrived disguised as tradition, respect, culture, and common sense. They were presented as natural, inevitable, and unchangeable. And when something is framed as natural, you stop questioning who created it, who benefits from it, and who pays the price for maintaining it.

One of the earliest and strongest expectations placed on me, and on girls like me, was silence. Silence was praised as good behavior. Obedience was praised as maturity. Compliance was framed as character. Speaking up, especially around boys, men, or elders, was considered improper. Even curiosity had to be carefully measured and softened.

Asking a question could feel like crossing a line. Not because the question was rude or aggressive, but because it challenged the assumption that elders were always right, that systems were always fair, and that things were always done for a good reason. A girl who asked questions was often seen as difficult. A girl who accepted quietly was seen as virtuous. Another expectation followed closely behind silence. The expectation of becoming what people casually, almost carelessly, call wife material. The phrase itself was rarely explained, yet everyone seemed to understand it instinctively.

It hovered in conversations, in advice, in warnings, in praise. It was not a single rule, but a destination quietly mapped out for girls long before they understood what it meant to choose a life for themselves.

This idea existed in different forms across cultures, families, and communities, but its foundation was always the same. A girl's success was not measured by how deeply she understood herself, her interests, or her inner world. It was measured by how seamlessly she could fit into a role designed by others. A role that valued adaptability over authenticity. Agreement over curiosity. Stability over exploration. From a young age, you learned to observe yourself through this lens. Were you gentle enough? Patient enough. Accommodating enough. Were your opinions soft enough to be palatable? Were your dreams small enough to be safe? Even your confidence had to be moderated, shaped carefully so it did not come across as arrogance. You learned to dim certain parts of yourself not because anyone explicitly told you to, but because the environment rewarded those who did.

Ambition, when it appeared, had to be carefully packaged. It was acceptable only if it did not disrupt this imagined future. Wanting to learn was encouraged, but only up to a point. Wanting independence was tolerated, but only if it did not challenge existing hierarchies. Intelligence was admired, but only when it remained non-threatening. There was an unspoken boundary beyond which curiosity became inconvenience and independence became defiance.

Wanting more felt risky. Wanting differently felt almost forbidden.

I absorbed these messages slowly, through repetition and observation. Through what was celebrated and what was quietly discouraged. Through the stories told about women who were considered successful and those who were described as difficult, complicated, or unfortunate. It became clear that the safest way to exist was to follow the script closely and ask as few questions as possible.

School, in many ways, reinforced these ideas, though not always intentionally. Academically, I performed well. Particularly in subjects that were considered difficult, the kind that often carried the unspoken label of being better suited for boys. Mathematics, physics, chemistry. I enjoyed the challenge, though at the time I did not fully understand why. There was something grounding about numbers, about problems that demanded focus and rewarded persistence.

On a school trip

Doing well in these subjects placed me in a strange position. On the surface, it was praise. Encouragement. Opportunity. But beneath it, there was a quiet narrowing of choice. Instead of opening conversations about what I wanted or where my interests truly lay, my performance became a decision-making tool for others. Because I excelled, it was assumed I should continue down this path. That this path belonged to me.

Decisions were made for me, not with me.

I was admitted to one of the best schools, not because anyone asked what I dreamed of becoming, but because my scores made me useful. Useful as evidence. Useful as an example. Useful as proof that girls could do it too.

There was pride in that, of course. Pride in being seen as capable. Pride in representing possibility. Pride in knowing that my success challenged certain assumptions. But pride coexisted with pressure. Excellence did not come with freedom. It came with expectation.

The system did not ask whether this path aligned with my inner world. It did not pause to ask whether this was where I felt most alive. It simply assumed that performance meant preference, that success automatically translated into desire. That if you were good at something, you must want to build your entire life around it.

And yet, within this structure, I was given something invaluable.

STEM shaped the way I thought. It trained me to approach problems with patience rather than panic. It taught me that complexity was not something to fear, but something to work through. That problems rarely had only one solution, and that failing on the first attempt did not mean you were incapable. It meant you had not yet found the right method.

I learned persistence through equations. Through problems that refused to yield answers immediately. Through long hours of confusion that slowly transformed into clarity. I learned patience through failure, through the quiet humility of realizing that understanding often comes after struggle.

I learned that asking classmates for help was not a weakness. It was a strategy. It was a collaboration. I learned that different minds could arrive at the same answer through entirely different paths, and that none of those paths were wrong simply because they were different.

These lessons stayed with me long after the formulas faded. They became part of how I approached uncertainty. How I responded to difficulty. How I made sense of situations without clear instructions.

What I did not realize then was how deeply this way of thinking would later shape my approach to fear.

At that time, fear did not announce itself loudly. It did not feel like panic or terror. It felt like hesitation.

Like the subtle tightening of something inside my chest when I considered stepping outside expectations. The first fear I remember clearly was not the fear of failing academically. That kind of failure felt manageable, almost technical. You could study more. Try again. Adjust your approach.

The fear that stayed with me was different.

It was the fear of stepping outside what had already been decided for me. The fear of disappointing those who had invested in a particular version of my future. The fear of being seen as ungrateful for opportunities others did not have. The fear of choosing a path that could not be easily explained or justified.

I sensed, even then, that deviating from expectations came with consequences that were not written down. That success was not only about ability, but about alignment. About knowing which boundaries not to cross. About understanding that some forms of excellence were celebrated, while others were quietly discouraged.

This fear did not stop me from thinking. But it taught me to be careful about how openly I expressed those thoughts. It taught me to weigh every desire against the potential cost of being different. And for a long time, it made me believe that wanting something more personal, more uncertain, or more self-defined was something I needed to earn rather than claim.

Only later would I understand that fear was not a sign that I was on the wrong path. It was a sign that I was standing at the edge of one.

Remember the scholarship story where I chose another professional technological course despite my family and community's opposition? On the surface, it may have looked like a simple decision, but inside me, it felt anything but simple. It was the first time I consciously stepped away from a path that had already been approved, accepted, and celebrated. I wanted to change my direction, even though I could not yet fully articulate where it would lead.

The university that I chose did not follow the safe, well-worn route that people trusted because it had already delivered predictable outcomes for others. In choosing it, I was choosing uncertainty.

Suddenly, the invisible rules that had always surrounded me became painfully visible. They were no longer abstract ideas floating quietly in the background. They stood directly in front of me, firm and unyielding. This is not how things are done. This is not how success usually looks. This is not what people like you choose.

The questions came quickly, uninvited and relentless.

What if it did not work? What if I failed? What if I became the example people used to discourage others from trying?

Fear took on a new shape during this period. It was no longer just a vague sense of caution. It became detailed and specific. It played out entire scenarios in my mind, vivid and convincing. I imagined returning home without success to justify my choice. I imagined conversations filled with disappointment rather than pride. I imagined the quiet satisfaction of those who had warned me, the unspoken "we told you so" hanging in the air.

I imagined being labeled reckless. Ungrateful. Foolish.

More than anything, I feared becoming the first person to try and the first person to fall. There is a particular loneliness in that position. When no one before you has failed publicly, your failure feels heavier, more symbolic. It stops being just your own. It becomes representative. It becomes proof, not just of your limits, but of what others believe people like you are capable of.

Fear, in those moments, was not dramatic or emotional in the way stories often portray it. It was not loud or theatrical. It was practical. It sat beside me quietly, making lists. It calculated consequences with unnerving efficiency. It reminded me, again and again, that if I failed, the impact would not stop with me. It would reflect on my family. My background. My gender. My community.

Failure, I learned, is rarely personal when you are the first.

And yet, beneath that fear, there was something else. Something quieter, but far more persistent. A steadier voice that refused to be silenced. It did not promise success. It did not guarantee safety. But it insisted on honesty.

It whispered that choosing safety over truth would feel like a different kind of failure. That following a path simply because it was familiar would slowly erase parts of me I did not want to lose. That there were questions inside me that would not disappear just because I ignored them.

This voice did not shout. It did not argue. It waited.

I did not experience guilt for wanting more in a loud or obvious way. It was not overwhelming or dramatic. Instead, it showed up as constant self-negotiation. A quiet back and forth that played out inside me every day. Was I being selfish? Was I asking for too much? Was I allowed to want something different when others were content with less?

From a young age, I had learned not to ask for things without preparation. Wanting something was never enough. You had to justify it. Support it. Prove that it was reasonable. I learned to come up with alternatives, solutions, and compromises already prepared. If I wanted something, I tried to show that I had already done my part. That I had thought it through. That I was not asking lightly or impulsively.

This habit followed me into this moment as well. I weighed every possibility. I calculated costs. I explored backup plans. I tried to reduce risk wherever I could, not because I doubted myself, but because I knew how easily doubt could be turned against me. Part of this came from awareness. I knew I was not the only child. I knew resources were limited. I knew that asking without offering something in return often led to dismissal. But this way of thinking also taught me something deeper, something that would later shape how I moved through the world.

It taught me to advocate for myself.

I learned to speak on behalf of my own dreams, even when my voice trembled. I learned to negotiate for possibilities that were not immediately understood or supported. I learned that wanting something did not make me irresponsible, but it did require me to be intentional.

I learned to negotiate for my dreams.

At the same time, I watched others conform. I watched people accept paths they did not question, not because they were deeply fulfilling, but because they were safe. Because they were familiar. Because they came with approval already attached. I watched silence getting rewarded and curiosity getting quietly discouraged.

I watched people choose certainty over curiosity, even when that certainty came at the cost of something unnamed but deeply felt.

And I felt an intense loneliness as I tried to imagine alternatives.

Trying alone is a particular kind of exhaustion. When you cannot share your doubts openly. When you do not know who will understand and who will judge. When you carry both the weight of fear and the responsibility of hope by yourself. It can make you question your own instincts. It can make you wonder whether wanting something different is a flaw rather than a signal.

In that loneliness, I often wondered if I was asking the wrong questions. If I were complicating something that did not need to be complicated. If conformity were simply maturity disguised as wisdom.

But even in my quietest moments of doubt, that steadier voice remained. The one that reminded me that imagining alternatives was not rebellion. It was honesty. That questioning did not mean rejection. It meant engagement. And that wanting to choose my own path did not make me ungrateful for what I had been given. It meant I wanted to use it to its fullest.

I did not yet know where that path would lead. I only knew that I could not pretend it did not exist.

Trying alone is often exhausting. Especially when you cannot share what you are trying to do with anyone, when you fear your ideas will not be protected, and when there is no one to say, "I understand why you feel this way." The internet was not as accessible as it is today back then. There were no quick search engines at your fingertips for reassurance. No anonymous space to ask whether doubt was normal. Even the few internet cafes that were available felt far out of reach for me.

I often wondered if something was wrong with me. I wondered if wanting more meant I was ungrateful. I wondered if questioning meant I lacked discipline. When things became difficult, there was no one to reassure me. No one to normalize the struggle. I sat with my doubts and tried to solve them the same way I solved equations. From different angles. With persistence. With hope.

One of the moments that made inequality impossible to ignore was a saying I had heard repeatedly growing up. A saying that declared, very plainly, *that a child is a boy*. Even if he is incapable. Even if he struggles. Even if he fails. The implication was unmistakable.

Being male was, in itself, a qualification. I saw this play out in real life. When my brother and I both had ideas, support came easily to him. Questions came later. For me, the order was reversed. I had to prove success before receiving trust. I had to demonstrate certainty before being supported.

At the time, it felt unfair. It required more effort, more preparation, more resilience. I felt as though I was constantly being tested. Looking back now, I see how it trained me.

I learned never to approach opportunities casually. I learned to research deeply, prepare thoroughly, and present ideas with evidence. This habit followed me into adulthood. It shaped how I pitch ideas, how I seek support, and how I protect my vision. What once felt like a disadvantage slowly became a strength.

During my Gap year

There were also moments when fear silenced me completely. During a long gap year between high school and university, I took a job promoting SIM cards. It was honest work. Simple work. Work that allowed me to earn my own money. But it was work that had to remain hidden.

No one explicitly told me not to do it. Yet it was understood that it was unacceptable. When I came home late one evening and found my father angry, I said nothing. I did not defend myself. My brother stepped in.

I remember thinking that I had a right to earn money. That I had a right to support myself when support was not provided. But those thoughts never reached my voice. Silence felt safer than truth. Fear, at that age, often expressed itself in awkward and almost absurd ways.

I remember falling asleep during evening prayers, dreaming that I was chasing a ball, and falling off my chair in real life. I remember waking up to punishment in the middle of prayer. Even now, I laugh at the strange logic of that moment. I remember hiding inside a mattress cover at school to sleep longer, only to be discovered and reported. I remember being questioned not for sleeping late, but for sleeping inside the cover, a rule that did not technically exist.

I remember stealing forbidden fruit, losing my glasses, and panicking more about the spoon in my pocket than about the act itself. Fear had priorities, and they were rarely logical. Fear, in my head, had many voices. Sometimes it was serious. Sometimes dramatic. Sometimes, almost playful. But its message was consistent. Be careful. Do not attract attention. Do not cross lines you cannot see. What I wish someone had told me then is simple. You will not die. You will go through this. You will survive it. You will learn from it.

Fear feels final when you are young. It feels permanent. In reality, it is often just another chapter. The first time I realized that invisible rules could be questioned was when I joined Scouts. It was the first space where curiosity was encouraged rather than punished. Where understanding came before obedience. Scouting taught me that discipline and exploration could coexist. Those rules could be questioned respectfully. Those problems did not have to follow one rigid structure.

It gave me a community where questioning was not rebellion, but responsibility. Slowly, I began to understand that invisible rules only function if you obey them without asking why. And that fear grows strongest in silence. If there is one thing I would tell a young girl who feels confined by invisible expectations, it is this.

Be yourself. Treat your life like an experiment. Try. Fail. Learn. Try again. The result will be worth it.

You are not broken because you question. You are not wrong because you want more. And you are not alone, even when it feels that way. Courage rarely announces itself. Most of the time, it begins quietly, with a single thought.

Chapter 3

Fear Wears Many Dresses

I *do not remember the first time fear announced itself loudly. I remember it arriving quietly.*

It did not come as panic or tears or something dramatic. It came as a question I could not shake. A small voice that asked, what if this goes wrong? It arrived before I had language for ambition, before I understood that wanting more could feel like a risk. Before I knew that desire itself could make you feel exposed. In those early years, fear did not feel like weakness. It felt like awareness. It felt like standing at the edge of something unfamiliar and sensing, instinctively, that stepping forward would change me. I did not yet know what that change would cost, only that it would not be neutral. Something would shift. Something would be asked of me.

I would feel it in moments that seemed ordinary on the outside. When an idea stayed in my mouth instead of being spoken. When I imagined a future that looked different from the one everyone else seemed comfortable accepting. When I noticed a quiet dissatisfaction with the script I was supposed to follow, without yet knowing how to rewrite it. There was no drama in it. Just tightening. A hesitation. A subtle pulling back.

At the time, I did not think of fear as something that needed to be conquered. I thought of it as something to be managed. Something to live around. It felt almost sensible, like an internal warning system reminding me to be careful, to not step too far ahead of myself. What I did not understand then was that fear was already shaping my imagination. It was teaching me where I was allowed to look and how far I was allowed to go in my thoughts. It was quietly drawing borders around possibility, long before anyone else had to. I noticed it most clearly when I imagined a life larger than the one already laid out for me. Not necessarily louder or more impressive, just wider. A life with choices that were not pre-approved. A life that did not come with instructions. Every time I let myself imagine that, something inside me would tighten, as if I had crossed an invisible line.

That tightening did not say no. It said, *be careful.*

And because it sounded reasonable, I listened. Fear, in those years, was deeply physical. It sat in my chest. It slowed my breath. It made my thoughts circle instead of move forward. It did not shout. It lingered. It waited patiently for me to reach my own conclusions. Often, fear arrived disguised as responsibility. As respect. As realism. It reminded me of where I came from, of what people expected, of the cost of making mistakes. It suggested that it was wiser to stay within what was already known, because known paths came with fewer explanations. I mistook that for maturity.

I had not yet seen that fear can sound like wisdom when you are young. Especially when you are surrounded by unspoken rules. Especially when no one explicitly tells you that it is allowed to want more. So fear did not feel like an enemy. It felt like a guide. A cautious one, but a familiar one. It kept me alert. It kept me observant.

It made me pay attention to the consequences. But it also made me shrink certain questions before they fully formed.

There were moments when I felt the tension between who I was and who I could become, without being able to articulate it. Moments when I sensed that something in me was capable of stretching beyond the frame I had been given, yet did not know how to do that without breaking something important. Fear lived in that tension.

It was present in the space between curiosity and action. In the pause before trying. In the silence after wanting. It made me rehearse possibilities without committing to any of them. And yet, even then, fear did not completely stop me. It only slowed me down. That is something I understand now, looking back with clarity. Fear was not trying to protect me from failure alone. It was trying to protect me from change. Because change meant losing the safety of being predictable. It meant being seen. It meant being responsible for my own choices. Fear arrived before logic, because logic comes from experience. Fear comes from instinct. It sensed risk before I could calculate it. It felt the weight of stepping outside the familiar before I could list reasons for or against it. It arrived before plans, because planning requires permission to imagine. Fear often arrives at the imagination stage, before anything concrete exists. It interrupts the dream before it becomes a goal.

It arrived before courage, because courage is not a starting point. Courage is something you grow into. Fear, on the other hand, requires no training. It shows up fully formed. What I did not realize then was that fear was already becoming a companion. Not a passing feeling, but a recurring presence. One that would change shapes as I grew older. One that would become louder in some seasons and quieter in others. One that would learn my patterns and adjust its arguments accordingly.

At that time, I thought fear would disappear once I felt more confident. Once I knew more. Once I proved myself. I believed fear belonged to beginnings, to uncertainty, to youth.

I did not yet know that fear evolves with you.

I did not know that as responsibilities grow, fear becomes more articulate. That as you gain more to lose, fear becomes more convincing. That it does not leave when you succeed, but instead asks new questions. All I knew then was that fear appeared whenever I imagined stepping beyond what was expected of me. It appeared whenever I sensed that my life could expand in directions that were not already mapped. It appeared quietly, persistently, without drama.

And because it did not announce itself loudly, I took a long time to notice it.

I took even longer to understand that fear was not a sign to stop. It was a sign that something mattered. That something unfamiliar was calling for attention. That I was standing at the edge of growth, even if I did not yet know how to step forward. Fear, in those early years, was not a barrier. It was a threshold. I just did not have the language for that yet.

Fear Has Many Faces

For a long time, I thought fear was one thing. Failure. That was the simplest version. The one people speak about openly. The one we all admit to, because it sounds respectable. But as I grew older and tried new things, fear revealed itself to be far more layered than that. There was the fear of failing, yes. But there was also the fear of succeeding too visibly. The fear of being judged. The fear of being asked, *who do you think you are?* The fear of being the first to try something no one around you had attempted before.

There was fear of rejection, often wearing the mask of realism. The fear of responsibility appeared only after the opportunity arrived. And then there was the fear of the unknown, the things I could not even imagine yet, but somehow felt looming ahead. Fear was not one voice. It was a chorus.

Sometimes it was loud and dramatic, turning small decisions into crises. Other times, it was quiet and practical, presenting itself as common sense. It whispered about money, timing, reputation, and safety. It changed its outfit depending on the situation. When I was younger, fear came mostly from the outside. From people. From circumstances. From watching what happened to others who tried and failed. From the environment I was growing up in, where stepping outside the expected path had consequences.

As I grew older, fear moved inward. It became informed by experience. By knowledge. By memory. By responsibility. It became internal, strategic, and almost convincing. Fear matured as I did.

When Fear Looked Like Logic

There was a time when fear pretended to be logical so convincingly that I did not question it. I trusted it. I let it lead. In my younger years, I was still trying to prove myself, not just to the world but to myself. I felt the need for everything I did to make sense on paper. I wanted my choices to sound reasonable, defensible, and intelligent. Ambition, on its own, felt too exposed. Too emotional. Too easy to dismiss. So I learned to dress it up in explanations. I needed reasons before I needed courage.

Whenever I felt drawn toward something uncertain or unfamiliar, fear would step in gently and offer structure. It told me that desire alone was not enough. That wanting more had to be justified.

Those dreams needed evidence before they deserved attention. Fear whispered that if I could explain myself clearly, then no one would think I was foolish. That if my choices sounded logical, then they would be accepted. That clarity would protect me from judgment.

At the time, this felt responsible. It felt mature. I was not afraid of failing as much as I was afraid of being dismissed. Of being seen as someone who did not think things through. Of being misunderstood and reduced to a stereotype of impulsiveness or unrealistic hope. Fear convinced me that logic was armor, that it could shield me from being questioned too closely. So I prepared explanations before taking steps. I rehearsed answers to questions no one had asked yet. I made sure I could defend my choices in advance, as if life were a debate I needed to win before I was allowed to participate.

In those years, fear did not sound like doubt. It sounded like discipline. But as my life grew fuller and my responsibilities increased, fear learned a new language. It stopped asking whether I was capable. That question no longer held power. Experience had already answered it. Instead, fear shifted its focus to consequences. It began to speak in the language of risk.

It reminded me of what I had built. A business that depended on me. People who trusted me. Stability that had taken years to create. It framed hesitation as protection, caution as care. Fear no longer questioned my ability. It questioned my judgment. It asked whether it was worth the risk. Whether I really needed to try something new. Whether the potential gain justified the possible loss. It held up responsibility as evidence, as if to say that wanting more was a luxury I could no longer afford.

And the questions it asked were difficult to dismiss.

Is this safe?

Is this necessary?

Do you really need to try this now?

These were not reckless questions. They sounded wise. Measured. Almost generous. They suggested that restraint was strength and that staying where I was could be a sign of maturity. Because of that, fear often won. It did not push me back with force. It guided me gently toward comfort. Toward familiarity. Toward choices that kept everything intact but rarely allowed anything to expand. What made this version of fear especially powerful was that it did not feel like fear at all. It felt like responsibility. Like adulthood. Like care for what I had already built. Only later did I begin to notice the pattern.

Fear was not asking these questions to protect me from harm alone. It was asking them to protect the status quo. It wanted to preserve what existed, even if that meant quietly postponing what could exist. Logic, I learned, can be used to build bridges or to justify staying still. Fear understands this well. It borrows the language of reason not to stop you outright, but to slow you down enough that the moment passes.

By the time you realize it, you are no longer choosing. You are maintaining. Understanding this did not make fear disappear. But it did change my relationship with it. I began to listen more carefully to the tone beneath the words. To notice when logic was serving clarity and when it was serving comfort. Fear still asks its questions. It still sounds thoughtful. But now, I pause before answering. I ask myself whether the question is protecting me or limiting me. Whether it is rooted in care or in avoidance. Whether it is truly about safety or simply about not wanting to be disturbed.

Fear can look like logic. But logic, when honest, does not silence growth. It makes room for it. That distinction took me a long time to learn.

The First Time Fear and Ambition Collided

The clearest memory I have of fear tied directly to ambition came in 2016. It was the first time I had an opportunity to go to the United States. It was through a program. There was a facilitation fee to pay, not a large one, but significant for me at the time. There were visa charges. There was the cost of leaving my shop for a month while still paying rent. My income was not high. I was already stretching to make things work. I did not have the money. I had to borrow for the visa.

What frightened me most was not just the expense. It was the uncertainty. The stories I had heard about visas. You pay. You apply. You are denied. You pay again. And sometimes you leave with nothing except disappointment. I kept asking myself if it made sense to borrow money for a visa. What if I did not get it? What if I failed before I even began? But I also knew something else, quietly and clearly. This opportunity mattered. Even if it was only a month. Even if it was only a visa. I knew it would open future doors.

Most people around me did not understand this. The question they asked most often was simple and practical. *If you cannot afford it, why are you doing it?* It sounded reasonable. It almost convinced me.

But opportunities do not always wait until you are ready. Sometimes they arrive early, demanding faith instead of comfort.

We went to the visa appointment as a group of ten. Because I got my documents late, I was the last in line.

In the US at Northwood University in Dallas

One by one, the first eight people were denied. I watched each refusal quietly. My fear grew heavier with every person who walked away disappointed. We were applying for the same program. We had the same letters. The ninth person was approved. People whispered explanations. She worked for an organization that often got visas. It made sense, they said. I was the last. I remember standing there knowing that if I failed, there would be no second attempt. No more borrowing. No more chances. When I was approved, relief came before joy. Fear did not leave. It only shifted its position. Now I had to go.

After the visa came the facilitation fee. I paid for it. To make the trip possible, I sold some of my household equipment. By the time I was traveling, I had the equivalent of two dollars with me. It was my first time leaving Africa. My first time traveling that far. I knew how it looked. I knew how it sounded. Even to myself, it felt almost irresponsible. But fear was no longer an excuse. It had become a condition. I told myself that I could not afford to mess up. That there was no backup plan. That I had to be careful, alert, and respectful. I avoided anything that could get me into trouble. I asked questions constantly. I made sure I did not break rules I did not fully understand. I was protecting myself, but I was also pushing past who I thought I was. I was doing things my personality was not trained for. Asking for help. Being visible. Admitting need. And underneath all of it, there was one grounding thought. *Even if this does not work, I will know I tried everything.*

That mattered more than success.

Fear was loudest before I began. Once I started, something else took over. Pressure replaced panic. Responsibility drowned out doubt. When you know you cannot afford to fail, fear becomes less dramatic. It becomes practical. I learned that fear often screams the loudest when nothing has happened yet. When the future is still imagined. Once action begins, fear loses its imagination. Bravery, I learned, does not feel like confidence. It feels like moving forward without guarantees.

A Funny Way Fear Made Me Behave

Fear does not always arrive as panic or paralysis. Sometimes it makes you behave in ways that are quietly ridiculous. You do not notice it at the moment, because you are too busy trying to survive with dignity. During that same program in the United States, our schedule was divided into two parts. The first part involved learning sessions. The second part involved spending time with a mentor, visiting companies, moving from place to place, and observing how things worked. We were often together, always moving, always surrounded by newness.

My colleague loved shopping. Whenever she wanted to go somewhere, the group went together. It was never really a question. If one person wanted to shop, everyone followed. I never wanted to shop, but I went along quietly. It was easier to blend in than to explain myself. One day, the mentor noticed. She asked me, almost casually, why I never bought anything. Did I not want to take gifts back home? Her question was gentle, but it landed heavily. I smiled and gave a vague answer, avoiding the truth that felt too exposed to say out loud.

The truth was simple. I could not afford to buy anything. Money was something I was constantly aware of during that trip.

I measured every movement, every choice, every desire against what I could realistically sustain. I was not there to collect souvenirs. I was there to learn, to observe, to absorb as much as I could without drawing attention to what I lacked.

Then one day, we visited a Facebook shop. As we walked through, my eyes caught on a jumper. It was not the style that held me. It was the textile. The craftsmanship. The way the material was constructed. At that time, my own shop was focused on clothing and textiles, and my curiosity was professional, almost academic. I wanted to understand how it was made. What it could teach me.

I lingered for a moment too long. The jumper was expensive. In my mind, it was completely out of reach. I had no intention of buying it. I did not even allow myself to consider it as something I could own. It was simply something to look at, to learn from, to remember. The mentor noticed my interest. Before I could explain, she paid for it. I remember the rush of emotions that followed. Gratitude, embarrassment, discomfort, relief, all tangled together. I thanked her, of course, but inside, something shifted. Fear recalculated. From that moment on, I decided that the safest way to move through the rest of the trip was to appear uninterested in everything. If interest could lead to generosity, and generosity could lead to discomfort, then disinterest felt like protection.

So I stopped looking. I avoided eye contact with objects. I walked through stores as if nothing existed. My body language became strangely deliberate, as though curiosity itself were dangerous. If the group stopped somewhere, I stood slightly apart. I trained myself to look neutral, almost bored. I must have looked absurd.

At the time, it felt necessary. I was trying to preserve a sense of control. I did not want to put anyone in a position where they felt compelled to help me again. I did not want to owe anyone anything. Fear convinced me that wanting, even silently, could become a burden to someone else. Later, the mentor laughed about it. She told me how obvious it was. I had gone from curious to completely uninterested overnight. How my effort to hide my desire had made it more visible.

Hearing it then, I laughed too. Looking back, it is genuinely funny. The way fear turned me into someone trying so hard not to want. The way survival disguised itself as indifference. The way I mistook restraint for strength. But at the time, it was not a comedy. It was instinct. It was fear doing what fear does best, adapting quickly, finding new ways to protect you from vulnerability. That experience stayed with me because it revealed something important. Fear does not always stop you from moving forward. Sometimes it simply teaches you how to shrink quietly. How to minimize needs. How to make yourself easier to accommodate. Recognizing that pattern, even through humor, was its own kind of growth.

Now, when I catch myself trying too hard not to want something, I pause. I remember that jumper. I remember how fear dressed itself up as politeness and practicality. And I remind myself that curiosity is not a flaw. Sometimes fear makes you cautious. Sometimes it makes you careful. And sometimes, it just makes you walk through a store pretending nothing exists. That, too, is part of the journey.

What surprised me most after taking that step was not the hardship. It was the support. I learned that resources are not only money. People are resources. Community is a resource. Humility is a resource.

Everywhere I went, someone noticed. Someone helped. Someone offered guidance, connection, or kindness. I did not lack anything essential. Fear had convinced me that lack of money meant lack of support. Experience taught me otherwise.

Looking back, I wish someone had told me earlier that fear needs to be named. When you do not name it, you do not know how to deal with it. You apply the wrong strategies. You think you are afraid of one thing when it is actually something else. For a long time, I thought I was afraid of public speaking. But what I was really afraid of were the words spoken to me when I was younger. The voices that told me I spoke too much. That I should be quieter. Once I named that, I could separate truth from memory. Naming fear gives you power. It turns confusion into clarity.

What I Would Tell a Girl Afraid to Try

I would tell her this. You might be the first to try *your* thing, but you are not the first to try something new. Every invention, every idea, every path once belonged to someone who went first. Connect to why you want to try. Not how. The *how* will change. The *why* will keep you moving. And ask yourself what happens if you do not try. What is lost then? Fear will always come dressed differently. But it does not mean stop. It means pay attention. Fear has walked with me in many forms. It shouted. It has whispered. It has disguised itself as wisdom and dressed itself as caution. But it has never stopped me. It has only asked me to choose.

And every time, even with trembling hands, I chose to walk anyway.

CHAPTER 4

The First Step Is Always the Loudest

The day everything shifted did not look important while it was happening. It did not announce itself. No one marked it on a calendar or took a photograph. If you had walked past me then, you would have seen nothing extraordinary. Just a young woman going about her day, carrying her thoughts quietly, appearing exactly where she was expected to be. But inside me, something cracked open. The first step did not arrive with applause. It arrived softly, almost apologetically, wrapped inside an ordinary moment. There was no dramatic confrontation, no bold declaration, no scene worthy of retelling. And yet, it carried more weight than any public milestone I had known. It was heavy in the way private decisions are heavy, the kind that settles into your bones before you even know how to explain them.

From the outside, nothing changed. From the inside, everything was loud. By then, I had spent years moving along a path that looked correct but felt strangely still. I had studied information technology. I had moved through universities, shifted programs, adapted again and again. I had collected certificates wherever I could find them, stacking proof of effort like small shields against doubt. I had done what was asked of me, and then done a little more, and then waited. And waited.

There were always papers missing. Always something delayed. Always another requirement that appeared just when I thought I was done. It was as if my progress depended on invisible approvals that arrived late or not at all. Each step forward felt temporary, provisional, dependent on someone else deciding that I was allowed to stand there. At first, I told myself this was normal. That patience was part of the process. That everyone went through uncertainty. But over time, a different feeling crept in. Fatigue, not of the body, but of the spirit. A tiredness that sleep could not fix. I began to notice that the exhaustion was not coming from the work itself. I liked learning. I liked building skills. I liked understanding how systems functioned. What drained me was the constant sense of waiting to be validated. Waiting for a stamp, a signature, a nod of approval that would finally say, yes, you belong here.

Somewhere in that waiting, I realized something uncomfortable. I was not tired because I was failing. I was tired because I was trying to succeed inside a structure that did not know what to do with me. The system was not designed for someone like me. Or perhaps it was not designed to be questioned. Either way, I felt like a shape being pressed into a mold that did not quite fit. The more I tried to adjust myself, the more resistance I felt.

I remember noticing how often my thoughts wandered away from employment. While others spoke about jobs with certainty, about salaries and stability and titles, my mind drifted toward possibility. Not ambition in the loud sense, but curiosity. What if there was another way to build a life? What if work could be something I shaped, rather than something I waited to be admitted into? That question scared me.

Choosing a job felt responsible. Choosing something undefined felt dangerous. I had been raised, like many others, to value safety, predictability, and visible progress. A job was proof that you were doing well. Starting something of your own was a risk people took only when they had backups, money, and connections. I had none of those.

And yet, the idea refused to leave me. It followed me quietly, showing up in moments when I least expected it. While walking. While sitting in class. While staring at documents that once again needed correction. It was not a grand vision. It was simply the thought that maybe I did not have to keep waiting. The moment itself was unremarkable. I did not wake up one morning feeling confident. I did not feel brave. I felt honest.

I told myself a single sentence. I am going to start something of my own instead of looking for a job. That was all. No fireworks followed. No rush of certainty. Just a strange stillness, followed by fear. Fear of what I had just allowed myself to consider. Fear of what would happen if I failed. Fear of how this would look to the people who cared about me. And beneath all of that, relief.

Relief that I had finally named what my body and mind had been trying to tell me for a long time. Relief that I no longer had to pretend I was waiting patiently when in truth I was slowly shrinking. Relief that the next step, though unclear, would be mine. It was not a rebellious decision. It was not made to prove a point. It was made because continuing as I was felt heavier than the risk of changing direction.

What surprised me most was how quiet the choice was. I had imagined that a decision of this magnitude would feel dramatic, like standing on the edge of a cliff. Instead, it felt like setting something down. Like releasing a burden I had been carrying without questioning whether it belonged to me. Still, the noise came later.

Once the sentence had been spoken inside me, my thoughts erupted. What if this were foolish? What if I was romanticizing struggle? What if this was simply avoidance, dressed up as courage? Who did I think I was, choosing uncertainty when so many people would give anything for stability? These questions did not arrive gently. They came in waves, crashing into each other, demanding answers I did not yet have.

But something else was present too. A quiet resolve. Not confidence, but commitment. I had said the sentence. I could not unhear it. I could not pretend I had not crossed an internal line. I understood then that the first step is always the loudest, not because the world reacts, but because you do. Because it forces you to confront yourself without the comfort of distraction. Because it asks you to stand by a choice before it has proven itself worthy.

Nothing in my external life changed that day. I did not resign from anything. I did not announce a venture. I did not suddenly know what I was building. All that changed was my orientation. I stopped facing the door marked approval and turned, slowly, toward the unknown. Looking back, I see that moment as the beginning of ownership. Not ownership of a business or an idea, but ownership of direction. For the first time, I was not waiting to be chosen. I was choosing. That choice did not make my life easier. It made it clearer. And clarity, I learned, is far more disruptive than confusion. The day everything shifted passed quietly. But it changed me. And once changed, I could not go back to moving through my life as though it belonged to someone else.

Choosing a Path No One Expected

Around me, the script was simple and universally accepted. You study, you graduate, you find a job. You earn a salary, you settle into a rhythm, you build something that resembles stability. Security was spoken about with the seriousness of a virtue, almost like proof of good character. A full-time job was not just work. It was adulthood. Responsibility. Evidence that you were doing life the right way.

I listened to those conversations and nodded along, but something in me remained unconvinced. The promise felt distant, almost theoretical. Not because I rejected the idea of work, but because the path toward it was never smooth for me. My journey through education was marked by interruptions, delays, and constant negotiation. Diplomas did not arrive when they were meant to. Examinations were scheduled in ways that felt impossible to manage. Each achievement came with an asterisk, each step forward followed by a reminder that it could be taken away.

There were moments when guidance would have made all the difference, but instead, I met authority that leaned toward intimidation. Administrators who made it clear, sometimes without words, that my presence was inconvenient. At one point, the truth was stated plainly. As long as a particular person remained at the university, I would not graduate there. It was said without drama, almost casually, and that was what made it so heavy. A single sentence, delivered without emotion, capable of undoing years of effort.

That sentence stayed with me. It echoed in quiet moments, shaping how I understood the system I was trying to succeed within. I began to see how fragile my position was, how dependent my progress was on forces I could not influence. No matter how hard I worked, there would always be something unresolved, something pending, something unfinished.

And yet, in the background of that uncertainty, another idea was forming. Slowly. Carefully. Almost shyly. I began to wonder if life had to be built entirely around employment. If the papers were always going to be uncertain, maybe I needed to create something that did not require me to prove myself at every turn. Maybe my value did not live solely in documents that could be delayed, denied, or dismissed.

I took stock of what I actually had. Skills I had learned through practice. Knowledge gained outside lecture halls. Experience gathered through internships, projects, and curiosity. My proof did not sit neatly in a file. It lived in my bag, in my laptop, in the work I could show, explain, and build.

The thought unsettled me. It challenged everything I had been taught about safety and success. It felt risky, even irresponsible. But it also felt true. For the first time in a long while, I was not imagining a future that required permission. I was imagining one that asked only for effort.

That honesty frightened me. And at the same time, it felt like the first real beginning.

The decision to start a business did not happen overnight. It grew slowly, over two years of internal negotiation. I took part-time jobs, short contracts, anything that helped me survive while I experimented quietly. I built a website. I wrote articles. I explored ideas without naming them as plans, because naming them would make them real, and real things attract judgment. I remember one birthday clearly. I had gone to church, feeling grateful simply to be alive and still trying. I was twenty-three. My bag, the one that carried all my certificates and documents, tore that day. Papers slipped out. Some were lost. Strangely, I did not panic. I felt a calm conviction settle over me. If even the certificates could disappear, then perhaps I was not meant to build my future around proving that I had them. By the time I completed university, my mind was made up. I would start something of my own. Not because it was glamorous, but because it was necessary. I did not feel secure enough to chase employment, and I did not feel willing to return to school again just to collect another piece of paper. I wanted to build forward, not circle back.

January 2014

There are dates that pass without leaving a mark, and then there are dates that quietly rearrange your life. January 2014 falls into the second category. It did not announce itself as a turning point when it arrived, but it has stayed with me ever since, clear and unmistakable, like a line drawn across time. Until then, I had been living in negotiation with myself. I worked on my idea in the margins of my life, in the hours that remained after survival. If an opportunity appeared, I would follow it. If a job offered stability, I would consider it. I told myself this balance was practical, even wise. One foot in safety, one foot in possibility. It sounded reasonable. It sounded adult.

In reality, it was exhausting. Every decision felt conditional. Every step forward was accompanied by a backward glance. I was never fully present in what I was building because part of me was always prepared to abandon it if something more acceptable appeared. The dream was treated like a fragile thing, allowed to exist only as long as it did not interfere with responsibility. In January 2014, I stopped doing that.

The decision was quiet and deeply personal. I told myself that I would no longer take a full-time job. Not because I believed I was above it, and not because I had everything figured out, but because I knew what it would cost me. I could accept short contracts. Temporary work.

Anything that helped me survive without consuming my days and my energy. But I would not commit to something that pulled me completely away from what I was trying to build. To the people around me, this choice sounded reckless and unnecessary. Stability, after all, is the goal we are taught to chase, not the thing we deliberately turn away from. From the outside, it looked like I was rejecting security without a clear alternative.

From the inside, it felt like clarity. I understood myself well enough by then to know what comfort would do to me. A full-time contract would slowly quiet the urgency that had been pushing me forward. It would give me just enough reassurance to postpone my own dreams. I would tell myself that there would be time later, when things were calmer, when I was more prepared, when the conditions were right. Later is a dangerous word. It sounds patient, but it is often just fear wearing good manners. Later convinces you that waiting is the same as planning, that delay is the same as responsibility. Later stretches quietly into months, then years, until the thing you once wanted becomes something you talk about in the past tense.

January 2014 was the moment I decided not to give *later* that power over me. I did not feel fearless. I felt resolved. I knew the choice would make my life harder in some ways. It would bring uncertainty, criticism, and moments of doubt. But it would also give me something I had been missing for a long time. Direction. That month, I stopped splitting myself in two. I chose to stand fully inside possibility, even without guarantees. And once I made that choice, there was no pretending that I had not.

Around that time, I took a job that was meant to help me survive. The description was vague, but it seemed to combine many things I was interested in. Creation, organization, even fashion. On the first day, I tried to understand what was expected of me. There was chaos everywhere. People moved around in ways that felt aggressive, disrespectful, and unkind. I was treated poorly. By the second day, my body reacted before my mind could rationalize. I felt physically ill. My shoulders were heavy, my energy drained. That morning, when I sent the message saying I would not return, something strange happened. I felt light. Energized. As though my body had been waiting for me to choose myself. It was not an easy choice socially. I did not walk home proudly explaining why I had quit. I kept the story small. I knew how quickly narratives form, especially about young women who refuse stability. I knew the comments that would come if I failed. Still, I knew why I had left. I knew I was not meant to be there.

That job taught me something crucial. *Just because you own something does not mean you have the right to treat people poorly.* I promised myself that if I ever became a leader, a founder, a voice, I would choose to be better, even when I could get away with being cruel.

When I finally committed fully to my idea, it was not with confidence. It was with conviction. I did not have a detailed plan. I did not have a safety net. What I had was a sense that I could not keep living halfway. I wanted to create something that mattered. At first, the idea was simple. A platform that informed parents and helped them understand how their actions shaped their children. I believed deeply that most parents do not intend to harm their children. They simply lack information. I mapped everything I had. My background in technology. My experience in media internships, both on radio and television. My network of people who knew how to write, design, and code. I realized that even if I did not have money, I had community. That mattered.

Support did not come in grand gestures. It came in practical kindness. A journalist friend offered me a media card and promised to write articles. Another friend, a designer, worked without charging me, telling me there would be time for payment later. A classmate helped me troubleshoot technical issues whenever I was stuck. Someone else offered to print documents for free. The first proposals I sent out were printed by a friend who believed in what I was doing, even when she did not fully understand it. These acts anchored me. They reminded me that belief does not always announce itself loudly. Sometimes it shows up as a printed page, a shared skill, a quiet yes.

Doubt From the Closest Places

Support does not always arrive from where we expect it. Sometimes, the strongest resistance comes not from strangers, but from the people who love us most. The ones who believe they are protecting us, even when their protection feels like a tightening grip. My family was worried. Their concern was not unkind, but it was constant. They wanted safety for me in the clearest way they understood it. A job. A salary. Predictability. When I chose a path that did not offer those things immediately, they grew uneasy. Without asking, they sent job applications on my behalf, as though nudging me gently back toward what they believed was sensible. Each application carried an unspoken message. This would be easier. This would be safer. This would make sense to everyone.

I knew they meant well. Still, it hurt. Back home, the story about me began to shift. Friends spoke as though I was avoiding responsibility, always running somewhere, never settling, refusing to work properly.

The movement that felt purposeful to me looked like restlessness to them. The effort they could not see was interpreted as absence. I learned how quickly silence fills with assumptions. The hardest moments were not confrontational. They were quiet. The sideways comments. The lowered expectations. The sense that people were waiting for me to come to my senses.

One moment, in particular, stayed with me. A family health insurance scheme was being organized, something meant to offer security and care. When the list was finalized, my name was no longer on it. I asked why. The explanation was simple and delivered without hesitation. Since I have a company, it should provide for me. I remember standing there, absorbing the words, feeling something shift inside my chest. I still get sick, I thought. I am still human. Independence does not make you immune to illness or vulnerability. But I did not argue. There was no point. I understood what was really being said. This was not about insurance. It was about doubt.

It was fear, dressed up as practicality. A way of saying, if you have chosen this path, then you must carry all of its weight alone. A way of reminding me that my decision had consequences, even in places where care should have been unconditional. That moment taught me something I had not fully understood before. Choosing a different path does not only ask you to believe in yourself. It asks you to accept that others may not be able to walk with you for a while. That love does not always translate into support, and concern can sometimes look like withdrawal. That was the cost of my first step. Misunderstanding, when explanation no longer helps. Distance, when closeness feels complicated. Silence, when speaking, would only deepen the divide. I carried that cost quietly. Not because it did not hurt, but because I knew that retreating would not bring me closer to myself. And even in the loneliness of that moment, I understood something important. If I could stay standing there, without approval, without reassurance, then the foundation I was building might be strong enough to hold me. Sometimes, the bravest part of choosing your own path is accepting that not everyone will recognize it as courage.

People often asked me what my backup plan was. I did not have one. This was not bravery. It was realism. I did not have the papers to fall back on. I could not simply apply elsewhere if things collapsed. That truth kept me moving. When fear whispered that I might fail, I reminded myself that failure did not automatically mean retreat. It meant adaptation. Another idea. Another attempt. The absence of a plan B forced me to commit fully to plan A, even as it evolved.

My biggest fear was failure, but not only my own. I feared betraying the trust of those who had supported me. People who barely knew me had offered resources, time, and belief. I carried that responsibility heavily. What if it did not work? What if I disappointed them? There was also guilt. I missed family gatherings. I became unreliable in social calendars. My mother began to assume I would not show up. That hurt, even when I understood it. Building something new required sacrifices that were invisible to most people. It required choosing long-term meaning over short-term approval.

The First Signs of Possibility

What followed my decision was not the kind of success people like to tell stories about. There were no sudden breakthroughs, no dramatic turning points that made everything feel secure. What came instead was movement. Subtle, uneven, but unmistakable.

And after so long of feeling stuck, movement felt like its own kind of victory. Things began to respond, slowly, as though the world was testing whether I was serious. Media houses agreed to small exchanges. They offered space, visibility, and collaboration, asking for trust in return rather than money. A billboard partnership appeared, unexpectedly, the kind of opportunity I would not have imagined asking for. Industry professionals, people who had no personal reason to encourage me, spoke positively about the quality of our work. Their words carried weight precisely because they were unprompted.

Then there were the readers. They responded with enthusiasm that both thrilled and unsettled me. They asked for more content, more stories, more depth, without knowing how much it cost to produce even one issue. They did not see the calculations behind the scenes, the compromises, the long nights of figuring out how to stretch limited resources. They only saw what mattered to them, and that was enough. For the first time, I felt something shift. What I was building was no longer living only in my head. It existed outside me, in conversations, in feedback, in anticipation. It had an audience. It had a presence. It was real.

One moment, in particular, stands out with surprising clarity. I received an email about an opportunity I did not even know existed. A grant. A program that supported ideas like mine. Until then, my understanding of funding was narrow. Money was something you earned, borrowed, or sacrificed for. The idea that people could invest in your work without expecting repayment felt almost unreal. I applied without fully knowing what to expect. When the acceptance came, it landed softly but powerfully.

Being admitted into that fellowship changed how I saw myself. It was not the money alone, though that mattered. It was the validation embedded in the decision. Somewhere, someone had read my work, understood my intention, and decided it was worth supporting.

That realization stayed with me. It loosened something tight inside my chest. For the first time, belief did not come only from within. It was reflected back to me by people who had no obligation to believe at all. That moment did not erase doubt. It did not suddenly make the path easy or predictable. But it gave me a quiet confidence I had not known before. The sense that I was not entirely imagining things. That the effort, the persistence, the uncertainty were leading somewhere tangible. That was the quiet win. Not a loud declaration of success, but a gentle confirmation. A small, steady voice saying, maybe this is possible. Maybe I can do this. And sometimes, that is all you need to keep going.

The first step was not about success. It was about identity. By choosing to start, I became someone who had started. That shift mattered more than any outcome. The first step was loud because it disrupted expectations. It forced people to react. It forced me to grow. I learned that courage does not precede action. It follows it. You do not wake up fearless. You wake up uncertain and move anyway. With each step, fear changes shape, but it does not disappear.

When I look back at that moment now, distance has softened the fear but sharpened the truth. What once felt risky no longer appears reckless to me. It looks necessary. I saw a young woman who was not chasing chaos, but coherence. Someone choosing honesty over comfort, alignment over approval. I see trembling hands, yes, but I also see steady intention. The kind that does not shout, but does not retreat either. At the time, I did not know where the decision would lead.

I only knew where staying would keep me. Looking back, that knowledge mattered more than certainty. It was not ambition that pushed me forward. It was the refusal to keep living a life that felt borrowed. The first step did not fix everything. It did not solve my problems or answer my questions. In many ways, it made things harder. Life became less predictable. Relationships grew strained. Doubt found new ways to speak. Choosing your own path has a way of exposing every insecurity you thought you had already dealt with.

But it also gave my life direction. Before that step, I was moving, but without orientation. I was busy, but not grounded. After it, even when things were unclear, I knew which way I was facing. I knew what I was building toward, even when I could not yet describe it. Direction, I learned, is not about knowing the destination. It is about committing to a direction and allowing yourself to grow into it. With time, I have come to understand that beginnings are rarely neat. They do not arrive when we feel ready. They arrive when staying still becomes unbearable. And they demand courage not in dramatic moments, but in quiet persistence. In showing up again, even when yesterday was hard. In continuing, even when no one is applauding. If you are standing at the edge of your own beginning, unsure whether to step forward, I want you to know this. The first step will feel loud. It will echo in your mind long after you take it. It will attract doubt, both from within you and from the people around you. It may test your relationships. It may force you to confront parts of yourself you have avoided.

It will ask more of you than you feel ready to give. Take it anyway. Not because it guarantees success, but because it changes you. Once you take that step, something subtle shifts. The ground beneath you begins to respond.

New possibilities appear, not all at once, but enough to keep you moving. You begin to trust yourself in ways you could not before. Looking back, I am grateful for that first step. Not because it led to a perfect outcome, but because it taught me that my life could be shaped from the inside out. That courage is not the absence of fear, but the decision to move with it. And that sometimes, the most important thing you can do is take the step that no one else can take for you.

Everything that followed began there.

CHAPTER 5

Who Said You Need Permission?

There is a particular kind of disappointment that does not announce itself. It does not arrive as a confrontation or a clear refusal. It settles slowly, almost politely, and stays long enough for you to mistake it for normal life.

For a long time, I believed that waiting was part of growing up. I thought decisions were meant to mature through patience, that restraint signaled readiness, and that clarity would arrive from somewhere outside me. If I behaved correctly, explained myself carefully, and avoided unnecessary conflict, someone would eventually confirm that the next step was allowed. I did not think of this as seeking permission. I thought of it as being responsible. Nothing dramatic happened when that approval failed to arrive. There was no single moment of denial. Instead, there were conversations that ended before they began, questions answered vaguely, plans postponed without replacement. Time passed, and the future remained strangely inaccessible. Certain decisions seemed permanently out of reach, not forbidden, but never quite available either. At first, I assumed the issue was timing. Perhaps I was early. Perhaps I needed to wait until circumstances aligned or expectations softened. But gradually, a different pattern became difficult to ignore. The delay was not situational. It was structural.

Some choices were simply not meant to be mine. This realization did not come with anger. It came with clarity. I began to notice how often my intentions were evaluated before they were heard, how frequently my reasons were questioned without being understood. I noticed how decisions that appeared ordinary when made by others became complicated when they passed through me. Permission, I learned, was not about safety or preparedness. It was about control disguised as concern.

What made this difficult to articulate was the absence of explicit opposition. No one said no outright. Instead, there were reminders of responsibility, caution framed as wisdom, and silence where encouragement might have been. The effect was subtle but persistent. The action felt premature. Desire felt inconvenient. Independence felt inappropriate. Waiting became habitual. It shaped how I thought, how I spoke, and how I planned. Before making a choice, I learned to anticipate objections. Before wanting something fully, I learned to imagine the reasons it might be unwise. The internal editing happened automatically. Over time, I became skilled at postponing myself.

There is a certain discipline in that kind of waiting. It teaches you to manage disappointment quietly. It rewards you with a sense of belonging, provided you remain within acceptable limits. But it also creates a dependence that is difficult to see from the inside. You begin to measure your readiness by external reactions. You mistake acknowledgment for legitimacy. Eventually, the cost of this arrangement became clear. The longer I waited, the less confident I felt. Not because I was incapable, but because my decisions were never allowed to fully belong to me. Agency, when consistently deferred, does not remain intact. It erodes.

The realization that no one was going to authorize my life did not arrive as relief. It arrived as a responsibility I had not prepared for. If no one else would confirm my direction, every decision would carry its full weight. There would be no shared accountability, no external justification. That was unsettling. Obedience, for all its limitations, offers a kind of shelter. It allows you to attribute outcomes to the system rather than to yourself. Acting independently removes that buffer. It requires judgment without validation. It asks you to stand behind your choices even when they are misunderstood. The shift, when it came, was quiet. I stopped waiting for conversations to end differently. I stopped revising explanations that were never going to be sufficient. I stopped framing my intentions as proposals. Instead, I began treating them as decisions.

This was not a declaration of independence. It was an adjustment in posture. I acted first and informed later. I made arrangements without extended justification. I allowed myself to move even when approval was absent. Not recklessly, but deliberately. Not impulsively, but without asking for permission that had proven unreliable. What surprised me was not resistance, but discomfort. My own. Acting without endorsement felt unfamiliar. It required a kind of internal steadiness I had not previously needed. There was no immediate reassurance. No confirmation that the decision was correct. Only the knowledge that it was mine.

That distinction mattered. Over time, something shifted. Not in how others responded, but in how I related to uncertainty. I became less concerned with whether my choices aligned with expectations and more concerned with whether they aligned with reality. Practical considerations replaced imagined judgments.

Consequences became manageable once they were faced directly rather than anticipated endlessly. I also learned that permission, when granted too easily, is often unnecessary. People adapt faster than they object. What initially appears unacceptable often becomes unremarkable with time. The world resists change less than it resists indecision. Looking back, the most limiting belief was not that permission was required, but that it would eventually arrive. Waiting was not neutral. It was a decision to remain stationary in a system that benefited from stillness. Choosing to move without approval did not resolve uncertainty. It clarified it. Risks became visible rather than abstract. Responsibility became tangible rather than theoretical. I understood, perhaps for the first time, that autonomy is not something you are given. It is something you practice.

There was no moment when I felt ready. There was only the recognition that waiting had become more dangerous than moving. That recognition was enough. I did not become fearless. I became precise. I learned to distinguish between caution and avoidance, between patience and delay. I stopped asking who would approve my direction and started asking whether I could accept the consequences of my choices. That question proved far more useful. Permission, I learned, is rarely a door that opens. It is a habit that must be broken. And once it is, movement becomes possible, not because the path is clear, but because standing still no longer makes sense.

Growing Up with Gatekeepers

In the environment I grew up in, decision-making was not understood as a personal right. It was a collective process governed by age, position, and tradition.

Choices did not belong to individuals; they moved through structures.

Authority flowed downward, and approval moved slowly, if at all. From an early age, it was clear that autonomy was conditional. Where you lived, where you went, how long you stayed, and what you were allowed to want were all subject to review. Even curiosity required restraint. Certain questions were acceptable; others were interpreted as signs of poor upbringing. Respect and obedience were not ideals to aspire to, but rules to follow. Curiosity, when expressed beyond narrow limits, was treated as a flaw rather than an impulse worth examining.

Good manners were defined precisely. They meant speaking less than you thought. They meant waiting, even when waiting produced no outcome. They meant recognizing when silence was expected and learning to occupy it comfortably. As a girl, I had stricter and more closely observed rules. You were permitted to exist easily only within clearly defined boundaries. Belonging was possible, but conditional. Ambition was tolerated, but only if it remained discreet. Permission functioned as a measure of credibility. Without it, your actions were open to doubt from anyone, including those with no insight into your circumstances. Approval worked as a form of legitimacy. If it was missing, your decisions appeared questionable by default. Motives were scrutinized. Competence was assumed absent. Independence, without endorsement, was interpreted as recklessness.

These rules were rarely explained. They were absorbed through repetition. I noticed early on that certain allowances were unevenly distributed. My sisters could stay overnight in other homes without discussion. They were welcomed, encouraged to remain, and treated as though their presence was unremarkable. I was always brought back.

Visits ended earlier. Stays were shortened or denied altogether. No clear reason was ever given.

As a child, I did not question it directly. Instead, I internalized it. Each time it happened, I assumed there must be something about me that required closer monitoring. Something that needed to be contained. I learned to associate restriction with personal deficiency rather than structural decision-making.

This pattern repeated often enough to become familiar. Over time, it ceased to feel exceptional. It became the background. What remained was a quiet vigilance. An awareness that presence had limits. That comfort was provisional. That staying too long required justification. Even now, long after those rules have lost their authority, the habits remain. I notice how quickly I prepare to leave spaces where I am welcome. How uneasy I become if I stay longer than expected. Permission, once denied repeatedly, leaves traces. It reshapes instinct. These were not lessons taught explicitly. They were learned through observation and correction. Through watching what was allowed and what was quietly discouraged. Through noticing which behaviors passed without comment and which attracted scrutiny.

Eventually, desire itself began to feel inconvenient. Wanting more space, more freedom, or more independence required explanation, and explanation was rarely rewarded. Over time, I learned a more efficient approach. I stopped wanting what I was not allowed to have. Or, more accurately, I convinced myself that I did not want it. This is how obedience sustains itself. It does not rely on constant enforcement. It teaches you to regulate yourself. To preempt conflict by adjusting desire before it is expressed. To interpret restraint as maturity.

There is a particular kind of discipline involved in this process. It produces individuals who are capable, adaptable, and deeply attuned to expectations. It also produces hesitation. Decisions are delayed not because they are unwise, but because they have not been authorized. Confidence becomes dependent on recognition. Action feels incomplete without endorsement. The most effective gatekeepers are not those who deny outright, but those who create systems in which asking becomes exhausting. Over time, compliance appears easier than resistance. Waiting feels reasonable. Silence feels responsible. Looking back, what stands out is not the severity of the restrictions, but their persistence. They were small enough to appear harmless, yet consistent enough to shape behavior. They did not prevent movement entirely. They redirected it. They narrowed the range of what felt permissible.

The effect was cumulative. Choice became something to be negotiated rather than assumed. Independence felt like something to be earned, rather than exercised. And by the time I began consciously questioning these patterns, many of them were already embedded. Growing up with gatekeepers does not always feel like confinement. Often, it feels like order. Structure. Care. But it also trains you to seek validation from the outside before seeking clarity from within. It delays the development of authority over your own life.

That understanding did not arrive suddenly. It emerged gradually, as I began to notice how much of my behavior was shaped by rules that no longer existed, enforced by people who no longer had control, justified by explanations that no longer held. The boundaries were gone. The instincts remained. And unlearning them required more effort than following them ever did.

Waiting feels polite. Safe. Responsible. It allows you to believe you are doing the right thing while quietly postponing your own life. I waited for approval to travel. To move. To choose differently. To try things that did not fit the expected path. Every time I asked, the answer was unclear or discouraging or wrapped in concern. Eventually, I noticed a pattern. For many things, permission was not delayed. It was unavailable. So I began doing things without asking. Not out of rebellion, but out of necessity. I travelled without approval. I moved without consensus. I registered for programs without long discussions. I informed people after decisions were already made. It was not boldness that drove me. It was exhausting. I was tired of explaining my existence. The shift was subtle but decisive. I stopped asking, "Can I?" and started saying, "I am going."

The First Time I Chose Myself

One of the clearest indicators that something had shifted was my decision to live alone. In the context I came from, this was not considered a neutral choice. Living alone as a young woman was viewed with suspicion rather than curiosity. The expected arrangement was clear. If you worked in the city, you stayed with a family. You remained there until marriage, at which point the transition was socially legible. Anything outside this sequence invited questions. Independence was not treated as an achievement. It was treated as a deviation. I initially followed the expected path.

Partly because it was advised, and partly because it was financially necessary. I moved between households, believing that proximity to family structures implied safety. It was a reasonable assumption, supported by social logic. In practice, what I encountered was silence.

At my first home

When boundaries were crossed, speaking carried consequences. If I raised concerns, the response did not focus on what had occurred, but on my presence. I was the temporary one. Others belonged. Any attempt to articulate discomfort risked being interpreted as disruption rather than self-preservation. The possibility of conflict between families outweighed the credibility of my experience. I learned quickly that being listened to was not guaranteed, even when something was wrong. In fact, especially when something was wrong. There was no formal instruction that told me to remain quiet. The lesson was taught through outcomes. Speaking led to displacement. Silence led to stability. Over time, the choice became predictable.

But predictability did not equal sustainability. Each move left something unresolved. Each adjustment required further accommodation. I became increasingly aware that remaining in these spaces demanded a steady suppression of my own voice. The cost was cumulative. It was not a single incident or a single household. It was the repeated expectation that endurance was preferable to departure. Eventually, the calculation changed. Staying no longer felt protective. It felt corrosive. I understood that leaving would introduce uncertainty, but staying would guarantee erasure. I did not want another explanation. Another compromise. Another arrangement that required me to endure discomfort quietly to preserve external harmony.

So, I decided to leave. The decision was not met with encouragement. It was met with interrogation. Why do you need your own place? Is your work stable enough to justify this? How will you manage the expenses? Why can't you do what others do?

These questions were framed as practical concerns, and some of them were valid. I did not have complete financial security. I did not have long-term certainty. What I had was clarity about what I could no longer tolerate. Leaving was not an assertion of confidence. It was an acknowledgment of limits. Staying had begun to compromise something fundamental. Not my comfort, but my ability to speak honestly about my own experience. Leaving introduced fear, but it also restored coherence. The decision aligned my circumstances with my reality. I did not leave because I was ready. I left because I understood that, in this context, readiness was being used as a moving target. It would always arrive later, under conditions that were never fully defined. Choosing to live alone did not resolve everything. It did not remove risk. It did not offer reassurance. What it did offer was ownership.

For the first time, my living situation did not require me to negotiate my presence. I did not need to justify staying or leaving. The responsibility was entirely mine. That responsibility was heavy, but it was also clean. I chose honesty over approval. Not because it was easier, but because it was sustainable. And in that decision, I began, quietly and without ceremony, to choose myself. Doing something without validation comes with a particular kind of fear. Not the fear of failure, but the fear of being alone with the consequences. When you choose without approval, you also choose silence. You do not complain easily. You do not share your struggles freely. You carry the weight quietly, because returning would invite a chorus of "We told you so." There was a time when I lived for weeks with almost no food. I had tea, sugar, and whatever I could stretch into meals.

When I eventually had money and ate properly, the hunger disappeared, but the fear stayed. Even now, I cannot sleep in a house without food. Not because I am hungry, but because I remember how it feels to lie awake knowing there is nothing to reach for. That fear shaped my relationship with survival. It taught me respect for stability and compassion for scarcity. I did not share that time with many people. Most would have told me to go home. My family had food. My family had space. What they did not have was room for the life I was trying to build.

Choosing myself meant choosing discomfort without witnesses.

I was not entirely alone. My sister supported my decision. Not emotionally loudly, but practically. She listened. She evaluated my plan. She reminded me that failure did not mean exile. That if things collapsed, I could return. That reassurance mattered. Not because I planned to return, but because it made the step survivable. Still, even that support came with the weight of approval. Moving from her home required an explanation. Logic. Planning. Proof. I learned that independence often begins with negotiation, even when it should not have to.

Questions Disguised as Care

Once the decision was made, the questions followed. They came from different directions and carried different intentions. Some were rooted in concern. Others were in fear. A few were shaped by anxiety about perception rather than reality. None of them was overtly hostile. That was what made them effective.

Why can't you commute like everyone else? What will people say about this? What if something happens? Do you understand how expensive life is?

These were not accusations. They were presented as practical considerations, offered in a tone that suggested responsibility rather than resistance. The language was gentle. The implications were not. Each question assumed a conclusion. That deviation was unnecessary. That conformity was safer. That the familiar, by virtue of being familiar, was superior. The underlying belief was clear. Stability existed inside established patterns. Anything outside them introduces an avoidable risk. Safety was associated with repetition, not intention. At the time, my circumstances were not abstract. I was completing my final academic project, beginning to build a company, and supporting myself through short-term work. These were not theoretical ambitions. They required proximity, flexibility, and time. I had reasons for my choices, and I articulated them carefully.

At first, I explained myself. I described logistics. I outlined costs. I clarified timelines. I responded to each concern as it was raised, assuming that understanding would follow information. I believed that if the reasoning was sound, resistance would soften. It did not. The questions returned, slightly rephrased but unchanged in substance. Each explanation prompted a new concern. Each clarification produced another warning. The conversation did not progress. It circled. Over time, it became apparent that the issue was not the quality of my reasoning. It was the premise itself. The decision had already been evaluated against a standard that did not include my priorities. No amount of explanation could reconcile that difference.

This was not opposition in the traditional sense. It was persistence framed as care. The insistence that safety required sameness. That deviation, regardless of justification, was a liability. Eventually, I stopped trying to persuade. Not out of defiance, but recognition.

Explanations do not always create understanding. Sometimes they simply extend the negotiation period without altering the outcome. Repeated justification can weaken a decision rather than strengthen it. Withdrawing from that cycle was not a rejection of concern. It was an acknowledgment of limits. I understood that reassurance had become a demand rather than a dialogue. The cost of continued explanation was not clarity, but erosion. I learned that some choices are easier to sustain when they are not constantly defended. That care, when filtered through fear, can become restrictive. And that not every question requires an answer. Silence, in this context, was not avoidance. It was a boundary. And within that boundary, the decision remained intact.

Living alone taught me things no one prepared me for. Landlords who assumed a husband would appear to pay rent. People who questioned my presence. Situations that revealed how deeply independence unsettles expectations. Instead of arguing, I learned to move. If a space did not respect me, I left. That freedom was new. In family homes, I had endured. Alone, I could choose. I learned what mattered to me. A place on a main road. Indoor bathrooms. Clear boundaries. Contracts. Independence teaches you through trial, not instruction. I did not try to correct everyone's assumptions. I built systems that protected me from them. That was power.

Not every choice was perfect. There was a time I stayed in a women's hostel run by nuns. It was safe. Structured. Predictable. And professionally suffocating. Curfews did not understand flight schedules. Permission was still required, just dressed differently. I realized that safety without autonomy was another kind of cage. I left again. Each move refined my understanding. Independence is not about rebellion. It is about alignment.

The biggest shift was internal. I stopped waiting to be believed. I stopped waiting to be understood. I stopped waiting to be validated. I learned that authority does not arrive as a gift. It is built through decisions, mistakes, and consistency. No one hands you permission. You give it to yourself, and then you live with it.

Self-permission is not always empowering. Sometimes it is deeply awkward. When I first started travelling alone, I shared every detail with my mother. Departure times. Arrival times. Every step. Her response was always the same. "Okay." That silence hurt more than resistance. I expected to worry. Questions. Emotion. I received neutrality. Eventually, I stopped sharing details. Not out of anger, but clarity. Care does not always look the way we imagine it will. That, too, was a lesson in independence.

What Permission Really Means

Permission is often presented as a safeguard. It appears rational, even ethical. It suggests patience, respect for structure, and consideration for consequences. In many environments, waiting for permission is framed as maturity rather than hesitation. But over time, I came to understand that permission can also function as avoidance. Not always consciously, and not always dishonestly. Sometimes it is simply fear made socially acceptable. Waiting feels responsible. It allows you to believe you are being careful rather than uncertain. It offers reassurance that someone else has evaluated the risk. But this reassurance has limits. When permission becomes a prerequisite for action rather than a point of reference, it quietly replaces judgment with delay.

I was trained early to wait. To listen before speaking. To adapt before asserting. To belong by staying within what was permitted rather than exploring what was possible. Obedience was rewarded with stability. Compliance was interpreted as character. There was nothing overtly oppressive about this training. It did not rely on force or punishment. It relied on repetition. For example. On subtle reinforcement of what was considered acceptable. Over time, restraint became instinctive. Desire was edited before expression. Action was postponed until endorsement felt likely. Unlearning this took longer than learning it.

The most difficult part was recognizing how deeply permission had shaped my internal decision-making. Even when external authority faded, the habit remained. I noticed how often I delayed choices, not because they were unwise, but because they had not been validated. How frequently I sought confirmation for instincts I already trusted. How easily I equated approval with correctness. Letting go of that framework was not liberating in the way independence is often described. It was destabilizing. Without permission, there was no buffer between decision and consequence. Responsibility could no longer be shared. If something failed, it would fail on my terms. That realization forced a recalibration. I stopped asking whether a choice would be accepted and started asking whether it was sustainable. Whether it aligned with my circumstances rather than with my expectations. Whether I could accept the outcome, even if it was misunderstood.

This shift did not eliminate doubt. It changed its location. Doubt moved inward, where it could be examined rather than negotiated. Fear remained present, but it was no longer deferred to others for resolution. I am still learning this distinction. Permission does not disappear all at once. It resurfaces in moments of uncertainty, in decisions that feel exposed, in situations where consensus would be easier than conviction. The impulse to wait has not vanished. It has simply become visible.

What has changed is the question I ask. I no longer ask who will approve of my life. That question assumes authority exists elsewhere. Instead, I ask whether I can live with my own choices. Whether I can carry their consequences without resentment. Whether the decision reflects clarity rather than compliance. That question is quieter. It does not offer comfort. But it produces something more durable. It produces ownership. And for now, that has been enough.

Chapter 6

When the World Says No

The first time the world said no to me, it did not arrive gently. It did not test the waters or soften its edges. It stood in front of me, unblinking, and spoke in a voice that echoed far beyond the room I was standing in. I remember the room more than I remember the people. It felt too big for the moment I was living, as if the walls had been stretched to make my smallness more visible. The air was thick with anticipation, the kind that sits on your chest and makes breathing feel like a conscious effort. My heart was racing, not with excitement, but with the fear of being seen before I felt ready to be looked at. It was my first time pitching in public. Not speaking in a classroom or a friendly gathering, but standing in front of strangers who were there to judge, compare, and decide. I was not only presenting an idea. I was presenting myself. My thoughts. My courage. My right to be in that space.

There was money involved. Real money. Fifty thousand dollars. Even saying the number felt unreal back then. It was not just a prize. It was a possibility. Rent paid without anxiety. Work continued without constant compromise. It was time bought back from survival. At that moment in my life, fifty thousand dollars did not feel like an amount. It felt like a mountain. Steep, intimidating, and standing between me and everything I hoped to build.

Until that day, rejection had lived in quieter corners of my life. It came through emails that never arrived. Through application portals that stayed silent. Through polite acknowledgements that meant nothing would follow. Those rejections were easy to tuck away. Easy to explain. Easy to ignore if I needed to protect myself. This was different. This was public.

People knew I was pitching. They had seen my name on a list. They knew there would be winners. And they would know, very clearly, who was not one of them. There would be no ambiguity. No private disappointment. No quiet processing in solitude. This rejection, if it came, would arrive with witnesses. At that time, I was still learning the language of business. My world had been shaped by stories, by people, by problems that needed attention more than applause. I knew how to speak about impact. I knew how to speak about need, urgency, and purpose. But numbers felt like a foreign dialect. Projections felt like predictions I was not confident enough to make. The vocabulary that others used with ease still felt heavy in my mouth.

Public speaking alone already carried fear for me. The fear of being misunderstood. The fear of sounding unsure. The fear of my voice betraying the uncertainty I was trying to hide. Speaking about business in public, with judges sitting across from me and competitors beside me, felt like standing exposed under a harsh light. I could feel all my insecurities gather at once. Fear of not knowing enough. Fear of not sounding credible. Fear of being the least prepared person in the room. Fear of being found out. When the pitches ended, time seemed to stretch strangely. There is a particular silence that comes before results are announced. It is not quiet. It is heavy. People sit straighter. Some avoid eye contact. Some smile too much.

I remember trying to slow my breathing, telling myself that whatever happened would be fine, while knowing that it would not feel fine at all.

When the results were announced, and my name was not called, there was no dramatic collapse inside me. No tears. No visible reaction. Instead, there was a strange stillness. As if something inside me had paused, waiting for instructions that did not come. I stood there, listening as others were congratulated, clapping when it was expected, nodding when eyes briefly met mine. Whoever was in that room knew what had happened. There was nothing to clarify. Nothing to explain away. The outcome was clear. When I left, I did not reach for my phone. I did not call a friend. I did not call my family. I did not say the words out loud. I lost.

Silence followed me home. Part of that silence came from exhaustion. Pitching had taken more out of me than I expected. It was not just the presentation. It was the emotional labor of believing in myself long enough to stand there and speak. By the time it was over, I felt empty, as if I had spent everything I had brought with me. Another part of it came from where I was in my life at the time. I was still explaining myself constantly. Explaining what I was building. Explaining why it mattered. Explaining why it did not look like what people expected. Each explanation felt like a negotiation, and I was tired of negotiating my own existence. But there was another reason I stayed quiet. One that took longer to admit, even to myself. I did not want to hear the sentence I already feared. I told you so.

I imagined it before it was ever spoken. I imagined it in different voices, wrapped in concern or disguised as advice. I imagined the looks that would accompany it, the subtle nods that said this outcome had been predictable.

I had not lost the pitch yet, but I was already tired of defending myself against conclusions that would feel heavier than the rejection itself. So I chose silence. That silence was not graceful. It was heavy and awkward and full of thoughts I did not yet know how to sort through. I replayed moments from the pitch. Sentences I could have said differently. Slides I could have explained better. Words I had stumbled over. I compared myself to others who had stood on that stage with confidence I did not yet recognize in myself.

But beneath all of that analysis was a quieter realization. This did not hurt, not because it ended something, but because it exposed something. It showed me how much I wanted this. How much I cared. How deeply I had tied my sense of possibility to a moment that lasted only a few minutes. That first public rejection did not break me. But it marked me. It showed me what it feels like to want something badly and be told, in front of others, that you will not have it. It showed me how vulnerable it is to stand behind your ideas before you feel fully formed. It taught me that ambition, once spoken aloud, invites judgment along with opportunity.

I did not know it then, but that moment was not just about losing a pitch. It was about meeting the world in its unfiltered honesty. A world that does not cushion its refusals. A world that does not explain itself. A world that expects you to decide, quietly and alone, what a no will mean to you. That day, I walked away without answers. Without validation. Without a prize. But with something else that would take time to understand. The knowledge that if I chose to keep going, I would have to learn how to stand in rooms like that again. How to speak even when my voice shook. How to hear no without letting it become the final sentence of my story.

The Echo of Doubt

Rejection rarely ends where it begins. The first no is only the opening sound. What follows is an echo, repeating itself in the mind long after the room has emptied and the moment has passed. It returns in questions, in comparisons, in a quiet but persistent voice that knows exactly where to press. After that pitch, the first question I asked myself was not strategic. They were deeply personal.

Am I doing the right thing? Am I doing it the right way? Am I even meant to be here?

At that stage of my journey, rejection did not feel like feedback. It felt like a verdict. If something failed, I did not separate the outcome from my identity. I became the failure. I replayed the pitch not to learn, but to punish myself. Every missed word, every moment of hesitation, every gap in my knowledge became evidence in a case I was building against myself. I questioned my preparation obsessively. Had I worked enough? Had I practiced enough? Had I misunderstood what was expected of me? I did not yet know how to ask whether the system itself was designed to favor certain voices, certain experiences, certain kinds of confidence. I only knew how to turn inward and blame myself. The room I had pitched in stayed with me in uncomfortable detail. I remembered the way others spoke, confidently using vocabulary that still felt new to me. They talked about numbers that lived far beyond my projections. They referenced technologies and models I had only recently begun to explore. Listening to them felt like sitting through a masterclass I had not prepared for, one where everyone else seemed fluent and I was still translating in my head. I compared myself relentlessly. Not in a healthy, aspirational way, but in a shrinking way. I noticed how easily others occupied space. How comfortably they spoke about growth, scale, and returns.

How little they seemed to question whether they belonged there. And with every comparison, I felt myself grow smaller.

The doubt did not stop at skills or knowledge. It crept into identity. I began to wonder whether I looked right for that room. Whether I sounded right. Whether my background, my focus on impact, or my way of telling stories instead of selling certainty marked me as an outsider before I even opened my mouth. I asked questions that had no clear answers. Was the rejection about me, or about the idea? Was it the timing, the model, the lack of polish? Or was it something unspoken, something I could not name but could feel in the distance between myself and those who seemed more at ease? There was a moment, quiet and unsettling, when I thought something that surprised me with its honesty. If I were the judge, I might not have chosen myself either.

That thought did not bring relief. It complicated the pain. The rejection felt fair, and that fairness made it harder to fight. There was no obvious injustice to point to, no clear mistake to correct. Just the uncomfortable truth that I was still learning, still early, still not as ready as others. And yet, fairness does not make rejection easier to carry. It only strips away the comfort of anger. What remained was a deeper doubt, one that asked whether effort would ever be enough to bridge the gap I felt so acutely.

I began to question my credibility more seriously. I was pitching alongside people who had technologies I admired, numbers I could only imagine, and experience that made mine feel thin by comparison. I remember thinking, very clearly, that maybe I should not be in that room at all. Maybe someone had made a mistake inviting me. Maybe I had overestimated my readiness. The doubt was not loud or dramatic. It was quiet and persistent, settling into everyday thoughts.

It showed up when I worked, when I planned, when I imagined the future. It asked whether I was building something that was truly needed or simply forcing myself into spaces that were not designed for me.

At the same time, there was a strange split inside me. I did not believe that I was incapable of growth. I could see that clearly. I knew I could learn, pivot, and improve. What I struggled with was the distance between where I was and where others seemed to be. That distance felt overwhelming. It made the path ahead look longer than I had prepared for. The doubt was amplified by the conversations around me. People questioned my focus. They asked whether I was in the media, in tech, or in fashion. They wanted a single answer, a clean label. My work did not fit neatly into one category, and that ambiguity made others uneasy. Each question felt like another reminder that I did not quite belong anywhere yet.

When things did not work, the explanation offered was always the same. You are doing too much. You need to focus. And every time I heard it, I wondered whether the rejection was simply proof that they were right. What I did not understand then was how much of that doubt came from trying to see myself through other people's expectations. I was measuring my worth using standards I had not chosen, in rooms that valued fluency over intention, certainty over curiosity.

In the aftermath of that pitch, doubt became a constant companion. It followed me quietly, asking questions I did not yet know how to answer. But it also did something else, something I would only recognize later. It forced me to look closely at why I was there in the first place. Not to justify myself to others, but to understand myself. At the time, all I could feel was the echo. The repetition of questions without resolution.

The sense that one had multiplied into many. But even then, beneath the noise, a fragile awareness began to form. Doubt, as heavy as it was, was also a sign that I was standing at the edge of something real. Something that mattered enough to shake me. I did not yet know how to quiet the echo. But I was beginning to understand that running from it would only make it louder.

The doubt inside me did not grow in isolation. It was reinforced by the confusion around me. That period of my life was marked by constant questions from others about what exactly I was doing. Was I in the media? Was I in tech? Was I in fashion? The answer was complicated, and complexity rarely makes people comfortable. I had started with a magazine, shifted information to a mobile application when print became unviable, and sustained myself financially through fashion. I was making clothes, especially for breastfeeding mothers, the same women I was trying to reach through media and technology. To me, these things were connected. Different tools serving the same people.

To others, it looked like a lack of focus. In tech spaces, people questioned why I was doing fashion at all. The media was seen as shallow. Fashion was seen as small. If I had technical skills, why dilute them? In fashion circles, people wondered why I bothered with media and technology when clothes were selling. In media spaces, visibility mattered more than sustainability, and no one wanted to talk seriously about money. Every time something did not work, someone was ready with a simple explanation. You do too many things. You need to focus. You should choose one path. Sometimes, they were probably right in ways I did not yet understand. But sometimes, their certainty made me doubt things that felt deeply true to me. I knew why I did what I did.

Fashion paid the bills. Media and digital platforms created access to information. Impact was the thread holding everything together. Yet, every slip, every rejection, made me question whether I was wrong to hold these things together.

The Quiet Moments where Giving Up Seemed Logical

There were moments when quitting felt reasonable. Not dramatic quitting. Just the slow kind, where you stop pushing and tell yourself you will figure it out later. I was tired of explaining. Tired of defending ideas that did not fit neatly into categories. Tired of feeling like I was always behind, always catching up. Sometimes I thought, maybe they are right. Maybe I should simplify. Maybe I should choose the safer option. The one that makes sense to others. The one that requires less resistance.

But beneath all of that was another truth. Stopping felt like abandoning someone important. The younger version of me who had started this journey with trembling hands and stubborn hope. I did not keep going because I felt strong. I kept going because walking away felt like betraying her.

What changed was not sudden confidence. It was clear. I realized that if I wanted to do business, I needed capital. And if I wanted capital, I needed to understand the systems I was operating within. I also realized that I did not want to sacrifice impact just to fit into traditional models of success. I had spent years learning by doing. Writing scripts, then studying photojournalism when I realized how much visuals mattered. Designing clothes, then learning sewing when tailors disappointed clients. Fixing problems myself because no one else would. But something was still missing. I wanted to grow. Not just sell. Not just survive. I wanted to prove that impact and sustainability did not have to cancel each other out. That realization led me to the Social Innovation Management Program. There were options in different countries. I chose India. It was the first cohort, and something about that felt right. New people, new perspectives, and space for questions instead of judgments.

For the first time, I felt like I was in a room where my confusion made sense. Where impact was not treated as a weakness. Where funding was not limited to one narrow path. I learned that there were many ways to raise resources. Many ways to sustain meaningful work. Many ways to tell a story. More importantly, I learned that I was not doing it wrong. I was just not in the right place with the right people. That realization was quietly liberating.

The Turning Point

The shift did not come with applause or certainty. It arrived quietly, almost casually, in the middle of a conversation that could have been easy to dismiss. I was sharing my confusion, my frustration, the sense that no matter how much I worked, people still seemed unsure about what I was doing. And then a facilitator said something that stopped me in my tracks. He told me I was letting people define me by my tools instead of my purpose. At first, it felt almost too simple to matter. But the more I sat with it, the more it unraveled everything I thought I understood about how I was presenting myself to the world. I realized that every time I spoke, I led with what I was building. The app. The magazine. The clothes. I listed them like items on a table, hoping people would connect the dots for themselves.

They rarely did. What people heard were products. Separate, scattered, sometimes even contradictory. They did not hear the problem.

They did not hear the people. They did not hear why any of it existed in the first place. In trying to explain everything, I was actually hiding the most important part. The facilitator went on to say something that felt both empowering and frightening. You get to decide the lens through which people see you. Until then, I had been reacting. Adjusting myself based on who I was speaking to. In tech spaces, I emphasized technology. In media spaces, I emphasized storytelling. In fashion circles, I talked about design and customers. Each time, I shifted slightly, hoping to be understood, and each time, I felt more fragmented.

For the first time, I considered that clarity did not come from simplifying my work, but from grounding it. I began to lead with the people I served. Women's health. Access to information. Dignity. Sustainability. I spoke about the gaps I had witnessed, the needs that were being ignored, the lives behind the data. Only then did I talk about the tools I used to address those problems.

The app became a tool, not an identity. The magazine turned into a phase, not a definition. The clothes became a strategy, not a distraction.

Something shifted almost immediately. Conversations changed tone. Questions became more thoughtful. People stopped asking me to choose between my projects and started asking how they connected. The story felt less defensive, less rushed. I no longer felt like I had to justify why I was doing so many things. I could explain why they belonged together. The confusion that had surrounded me, and that I had internalized as failure, began to settle. Not because everyone suddenly agreed with me, but because I finally agreed with myself. This shift did not make rejection disappear. I still heard no. I still faced skepticism. But the meaning of no changed. It stopped feeling like a judgment on my worth or the validity of my work.

Instead, it became information. Feedback. A signal of alignment or misalignment.

Some told me that the person across from me was not the right fit. Some told me that my timing was off. Some revealed that I needed to communicate more clearly, not work harder. And some simply reminded me that not everyone needs to understand what you are building for it to be necessary.

The most important change happened internally. I stopped absorbing rejection as proof that my work did not matter. I began to see it as part of the process of refining not just my pitch, but my sense of direction. Once I understood my purpose clearly, I no longer felt the urge to shrink or reshape it to fit every room. I could walk into spaces knowing what I stood for, even if I did not yet know the outcome. That confidence was not loud. It did not erase doubt. But it gave me something steadier than approval. It gave me orientation.

From that point on, rejection lost its power to define me. It could still slow me down. It could still frustrate me. But it could no longer convince me that I was lost. I knew who I was serving. I knew why I was there. And that made all the difference. That was the turning point. Not a victory, not a breakthrough others could see, but a quiet decision to take control of my own narrative. To choose purpose over presentation. And to trust that when the story is clear, the right people will eventually hear it.

Looking back, some of those rejection moments are almost funny. I remember dressing up carefully for meetings that lasted three minutes. Preparing pitches that never made it past the first slide. Rehearsing answers to questions that were never asked. Just last year, an organization that had once rejected me years ago invited me to make another pitch.

This time, the potential funding was not fifty thousand dollars, but up to two million. I laughed when I read the email. Not out of bitterness. Out of perspective. I sent a new pitch, but this time I did not twist my story to fit their expectations. I was no longer desperate for their approval. By then, I had options. I understood alignment. I knew what I was willing to compromise on and what I was not. Rejection feels lighter when you have choices. When one door closes, and you know there are others. When you understand that every no is meant to be challenged.

Rejection taught me that the world resists what it does not yet understand. That being early often looks like being wrong. That closed doors are not always permanent. Sometimes, they are simply asking you to knock differently. Sometimes they are redirecting you to a place that fits better. It also taught me that confidence is not about pretending rejection does not hurt. It is about not letting it decide who you are. I learned to rest without quitting. To pause without abandoning my purpose. To protect my work until it was strong enough to stand on its own.

This chapter is not about victory. It is about endurance. About staying long enough for your story to make sense. About learning that no does not mean stop. Sometimes it simply means not this way, not this time. And that is something I wish I had known earlier.

CHAPTER 7

Becoming the Woman I Needed

There was a form in front of me with too many boxes to tick and too many consequences attached to each signature. Consent forms do that. They do not care who you are outside the room. They reduce your life to checkmarks and initials. They ask you to accept uncertainty in ink. No metaphors. No reassurance. Just risk, stated plainly. I remember holding the pen longer than necessary. Not because I could not decide, but because the weight of the moment felt unfamiliar. It was not fear that slowed me down. It was awareness. A kind of stillness that demanded attention.

What surprised me was not the seriousness of the surgery. It was the question that surfaced in my mind. Had I done enough to leave things in order? It was not a dramatic question. It did not arrive with panic. It came quietly, like a checklist unfolding on its own. I did not think about legacy or grand meaning. I thought about responsibility. About whether the systems I had built could stand without me. About whether the people who depended on me would still be protected. The calm that followed unsettled me more than fear would have.

I had expected nerves. I had expected hesitation. What I did not expect was this steadiness. This sense of internal alignment. The kind that does not come from bravery, but from completion.

It took me a moment to understand where that calm was coming from. Weeks earlier, I had signed something else. It was not a form anyone would photograph. It was not a moment worth announcing. There was no audience for it, no symbolic weight attached. It was an invoice. Clean. Administrative. Precise.

Private health insurance. Not for me. For everyone who worked with me. I remember closing my laptop after the payment went through. No relief. No celebration. Just a deep, unfamiliar pause. As if my body had registered something my mind had not yet articulated. I did not call anyone. I did not tell anyone. I did not mark the moment in any visible way. But I stayed sitting longer than usual, aware that something had shifted beneath the surface.

It was not pride. It was not an accomplishment. It was the absence of a tension I had carried for years without naming. For the first time, I was not bargaining with myself about care. I was not weighing worthiness. I was not postponing my own needs under the familiar logic of "later." Something fundamental had settled. I had not realized how often I had negotiated with myself until that negotiation disappeared. There is a particular exhaustion that comes from constantly deciding whether you deserve something basic. It does not announce itself as fatigue. It hides behind discipline. Behind responsibility. Behind the belief that postponing yourself is the same as being strong. I had lived inside that belief for a long time. The invoice did not make me generous. It made me honest. Honest about what I had been waiting for. I had always told myself that I would rest later. That I would take care of myself once things were stable. That I would allow softness once everything else was secured. What I had not admitted was that "later" was not a time. It was a condition. A condition I did not feel I had earned yet.

When I paid for everyone's insurance, that condition dissolved. Not because I had become wealthy or invincible, but because I had fulfilled something internal. Something ethical. Something personal. Only then did I understand why the pen felt light in my hand at the hospital. The calm did not come from fearlessness. It came from closure. If something went wrong, I knew the work would continue. Not in abstract terms, but in practical ones. People would not be left uncovered. Decisions would not be stalled by uncertainty. The things that mattered most would not unravel simply because I was absent. That knowledge changed everything. It allowed me to look at the consent form not as a gamble, but as a choice. I was not signing out of desperation. I was signing from readiness. That distinction matters.

We often talk about courage as something loud. As something visible. As something that announces itself through bold gestures and decisive action. But this was not that kind of moment. This was quiet courage. The kind that shows up in preparation. In foresight. In making sure the floor is steady before stepping forward. Somewhere along the way, without planning for it, I had crossed into a different role. I had become the person who does not rush into bravery without protection. The person who understands that resilience without support is just endurance in disguise. The person who knows that asking someone to be strong without making them safe is not leadership. It is negligence.

I did not arrive at that understanding through theory. I arrived at it through repetition. Through years of watching how easily people are asked to sacrifice without being supported. Through knowing how deeply the absence of care shapes the way we move through the world. I had learned that lesson early. Too early. And now, standing there with the pen still in my hand, I realized something quietly profound.

I was no longer trying to survive the way I once had. I was operating from a different center. Not the loud kind of strength. Not the kind that demands recognition. But the practical kind. The kind that builds safety before asking for courage. The kind that understands that dignity lives in systems, not speeches.

I had become the woman I once needed. Not the one who stands in front and says everything will be fine. The one who makes sure it actually is. That realization did not make me emotional. It grounded me. I signed the form. Not because I was fearless, but because I was ready. Ready to receive the same care I had insisted others deserved. Ready to stop postponing myself in the name of responsibility. Ready to accept that protection is not a reward for suffering, but a condition for living well.

As I placed the pen down, I understood something clearly. This moment was not about surgery. It was about alignment. About the quiet satisfaction of knowing that when my body asked for proof, I did not have to search for it. I had already done the work.

The Girl I Once Was

When I think about my younger self, I do not remember ambition first. I remember the explanation. The constant need to justify why something hurt, why something mattered, why something was necessary. Health was never simple. Pain was never believed easily. From the age of fifteen, I lived with cramps that shaped my relationship with my body. Yet when I spoke about them, they were dismissed. I was told I was not the first girl in the house to experience periods, as if pain followed a hierarchy, and I had not earned the right to complain. I learned to doubt my own body before anyone explicitly told me to.

I thought this was normal. I assumed everyone lived like this. That everyone endured quietly. That this was simply the cost of being a girl. It was only much later, when I began having open conversations with friends, that I realized something unsettling. Not everyone lived in pain. Not everyone spent days each month managing survival. Some people did not even understand what I meant when I described my experience. That realization stayed with me.

Some needs should not require explanation. But mine often did. Sanitary pads were not optional, yet every month I had to ask for money for them. Over and over again. One dollar at a time. Eventually, the asking itself became the problem. One day, I was told to stop the thing that made me come back every month asking for money. I was seventeen. The money was not given. I remember standing there, confused. Not angry. Confused. If there was a way to stop it, I wanted to know. So I called my sister, who worked in the medical field. I asked her if there was a way to stop periods without getting pregnant. She understood immediately what I was really asking. She sent me the money and told me to stop asking questions.

Later, when another sister tried to give me money on behalf of the same person who had refused me, I refused it. Whatever I needed could not wait. And something inside me had closed. That was the moment I learned something dangerous. That honesty was not always rewarded. That sometimes, you had to ask for one thing to get another. That survival required a strategy. I hated that lesson. But I carried it with me.

There is a long, exhausting distance between surviving and becoming. Since 2014, I have carried a quiet promise. If I ever built something of my own, it would protect people better than I had been protected.

Not symbolically. Practically. From 2019 onward, that promise became a daily pressure. Friends would tell me I had achieved enough. That I could rest. That I had done well. But I could not rest yet. Because rest, to me, meant completion. And I was not complete until the basics were covered. Not just compulsory things, but necessary ones. Health. Security. Dignity. Private health insurance became the mark. Not because public healthcare did not exist, but because access, quality, and certainty mattered. Because queues were not just inconvenient. They were unpredictable. Pain does not schedule itself politely.

It took ten years to get there. Ten years of choosing raw materials over comfort. Ten years of postponing ease. Ten years of building toward something invisible but essential.

Choosing Others Before Myself

In 2024, I was diagnosed with fibroids. Surgery was mentioned as an option, not as an urgent step. Insurance, however, was not an option. I listened. I understood. I went home carrying the knowledge quietly. At that point, I could have chosen myself. I could have rearranged priorities, found a way, and taken steps sooner. Nothing was actively stopping me. But something inside me did. It was not guilt. It was not martyrdom. It was a line I could not cross without breaking something internal. I knew that if I took personal insurance before offering it to everyone else, it would feel like betrayal. Not of a principle, but of a younger version of myself. Of a promise I had carried for years without speaking it aloud.

I had spent too long trying to understand what it meant to need care and not receive it. I could not replicate that hierarchy in reverse. I could not protect myself first and ask others to wait. So, I waited. Waiting was not heroic.

It was inconvenient. It required discipline that did not look impressive from the outside. There were moments when the delay felt unnecessary, even foolish. Moments when people around me questioned why I was postponing something so personal.

But for me, the order mattered. Health is not just biological. It is ethical. It is relational. It is shaped by how we decide whose well-being comes first. Only when everyone was covered did I allow myself to begin my own health journey. That permission was not external. No one granted it. It came from alignment. From knowing that I was not taking something for myself that I had denied others. When the doctor discussed surgery options, I expected a familiar script. Private hospitals. Better services. Higher costs framed as better outcomes. Instead, he surprised me. He told me not to spend money unnecessarily. He told me to go where my insurance would work. He said healing mattered more than prestige. That sentence stayed with me. *Healing mattered more than prestige*. There was no judgment in his tone. No assumption about what I could or could not afford. Just a clear boundary between care and appearance.

When he explained that the surgery could be done anywhere, that it was not exclusive to a particular institution, I felt an unexpected relief. The decision simplified itself. This was not about comfort or image. It was about treatment. Through his recommendation, I went to a public hospital. I did not insist on privacy as a status. I did not frame discomfort as sacrifice. I chose care without embellishment.

The experience reminded me of something important. That dignity is not always tied to the environment. That quality is not always visible. That sometimes, the most ethical choice is the least performative one.

The moment that mattered most came later. After the systems were in place. After I knew that health was no longer a negotiation for anyone who worked with me. Only then did I sign my own surgery papers. The act itself was simple. Another form. Another signature. But this time, it felt different. I was not choosing myself at the expense of others. I was choosing myself within a structure that could hold everyone.

That distinction brought peace. There is a particular kind of anxiety that comes from being indispensable. From knowing that if you disappear, things collapse. That weight follows you everywhere. It turns even necessary rest into guilt. It transforms care into risk.

By the time I signed those papers, that anxiety was gone. If something happened to me, everything I was responsible for would continue. Not because I was replaceable, but because I had built something that did not depend on my presence alone.

People would still be protected. Health would not become an emergency simply because I was absent. Decisions would not stall in uncertainty. That knowledge was grounding. It allowed me to walk into the process without fear amplified by responsibility. It allowed my body to focus on healing rather than on contingency planning. For the first time, I was not bracing myself against consequences beyond my control.

I was simply present. Choosing others before myself did not mean abandoning myself forever. It meant waiting until self-care did not come at someone else's cost. That order matters. It is easy to confuse delay with denial. But this was not a denial. It was sequencing. It was choosing timing that aligned with values rather than urgency. When I finally allowed myself to care, it did not feel overdue. It felt earned in a way that had nothing to do with suffering. It felt complete.

Peace, I learned, does not come from putting yourself last indefinitely. It comes from knowing exactly when it is your turn, and stepping forward without hesitation. By the time I did, I was ready.

Sometimes the clearest mirror appears unexpectedly. During recruitment last year, I interviewed a young woman whose voice trembled as she spoke. She cared deeply about the work. So deeply that emotion hovered just beneath her words. I recognized it immediately. I remembered crying when explaining why I started my own work. I remembered worrying that no one would trust someone who cried while speaking about purpose. Sitting across from her, I felt tenderness instead of judgment. I did not need to know her full story. I knew what it meant to care deeply in spaces that reward detachment. That moment confirmed something for me. Becoming the woman I needed was not about having answers. It was about creating space where emotion was not a liability.

I still find it strange when people ask me for advice. I am the sixth child. I was never consulted for decisions. I grew up consuming what was decided, not shaping outcomes. Yet success changes how people listen. Entrepreneurs who started alongside me, then chose different paths, come back years later asking how to return. Some were told to marry early. To choose safety. To step away from ambition. I listen. I answer when I can. I do not see myself as wise. I see myself as someone who stayed.

Treating Myself as Worth Protecting

For a long time, the idea of caring for myself felt suspicious. Not indulgent, not lazy, not unnecessary. Suspicious. Rest felt like something that needed justification. Health felt like a luxury to be accessed only after everything else was taken care of. Joy felt conditional, as though it needed to be earned through exhaustion. I carried a quiet question with me everywhere. If I slow down, am I being selfish? If I choose myself, am I abandoning responsibility? That question shaped more of my life than I realized. It influenced how I worked, how I moved, and how I measured my worth. Productivity became proof of goodness. Fatigue became evidence of commitment. The absence of rest felt virtuous.

I did not question this framework for a long time. It had been handed to me fully formed. You work until you are depleted. You keep going until there is nothing left to give. Only then may you stop. But bodies do not function on moral logic. They do not recognize sacrifice as a form of strength. They respond to care, to attention, to consistency. When I began treating myself like someone worth protecting, it was not a dramatic decision. It was a series of small permissions. Small refusals. Small moments where I chose to listen instead of override.

The change was subtle at first. I noticed that my energy returned without effort. Not the artificial kind that comes from caffeine or supplements, but a steady, grounded vitality. The kind that allows you to move through a day without bracing yourself against it. My focus sharpened. Tasks that once felt heavy became manageable. Concentration was no longer something I had to force. It arrived naturally, as though my mind had been waiting for my body to catch up. And joy appeared quietly.

Not the loud kind. Not the kind that announces itself through achievement or reward. But the internal kind. The kind that sits in your chest and does not need an external reason. I realized then how long I had been fighting my own body. For years, I had treated it as something to be pushed, overridden, and negotiated with.

Pain was something to work through. Fatigue was something to silence. Signals were treated as obstacles rather than information. When I stopped doing that, everything shifted. I became better at my work not because I tried harder, but because I was no longer exhausted. My thinking became clearer because my body was no longer in survival mode.

Presence replaced urgency. I began to notice how much energy had been consumed simply by holding myself together. By ignoring discomfort. By suppressing need. When that resistance disappeared, there was space. Space for creativity. Space for attention. Space for ease. Treating myself as worth protecting did not make me less responsible. It made me more precise. I could distinguish between what truly required urgency and what was driven by habit. I could respond instead of react. I could rest without the internal noise of guilt. Responsibility, I learned, is not the same as self-erasure. There is a false narrative that care weakens discipline. That kindness softens resolve. That if you stop pushing, you will stop moving. My experience taught me the opposite.

Protection created endurance. Care created sustainability. Kindness created clarity. When I allowed myself to be well, my work benefited. When I allowed myself to be rested, my decisions improved. When I allowed myself joy, my resilience deepened.

The shift was not immediate, but it was consistent. I stopped asking whether I deserved rest. I stopped framing health as something to justify. I stopped waiting for permission to feel okay. This was not a rejection of responsibility. It was an evolution of it. I understood then that responsibility without care eventually collapses. That commitment without nourishment becomes brittle. That strength without protection is just prolonged strain.

Treating myself as worth protecting did not make life easier. It made it honest.

I no longer performed endurance for approval. I no longer equated suffering with value. I no longer mistook depletion for dedication.

Instead, I learned to listen. To the signals that told me when to stop. To the quiet cues that asked for rest. To the moments when joy appeared without explanation. These were not distractions from purpose. They were evidence of alignment. My body stopped resisting me. My mind stopped racing ahead of itself. Work became something I could engage with fully rather than survive. And in that shift, I understood something essential. Caring for myself was not selfish. It was strategic. It was ethical. It was necessary. It allowed me to show up fully, not just consistently. It allowed me to sustain what I had built rather than burn through it. Treating myself as worth protecting did not take anything away from the world. It gave me back to it.

Becoming the woman I needed did not mean arriving at certainty. It meant arriving at compassion. I no longer question whether I deserve care. I no longer negotiate my pain. I no longer apologize for needing protection. I am still becoming. I'm still learning. Still growing. But now, when I look back, I see continuity instead of fracture. The girl who endured quietly did not disappear. She evolved. Every time I choose care over neglect, trust over doubt, and honesty over fear, I honor her.

CHAPTER 8

Humor as Resistance, Laughter as Survival

I learned early that silence could be dangerous.
Not the quiet of rest or reflection, but the silence that follows a question asked by someone older, someone certain, someone who does not expect to be challenged or disappointed. In the rooms where I grew up, silence was never neutral. It carried meaning. It marked absence. And absence was read as failure. When the elders spoke, their words arrived, shaped by authority and repetition. Scripture was read the same way. Whole chapters, never fragments, never pauses long enough to ask whether the listener had followed or understood. The words moved forward whether you were ready or not. You were expected to keep up, even if your legs were shorter.

Silence in those rooms was interpreted quickly. Silent meant you were not listening. Not listening meant you were careless. Carelessness meant you needed correction. Correction, in my world, did not arrive softly. It arrived as a reminder that you were out of place, that attention was owed, that obedience was not optional. I was seven years old when I first fully understood this sequence. Not in theory, but in my body. Every evening, we gathered to read from the Bible. It was routine, unquestioned, as ordinary as the time of day. The book was heavy, both in weight and expectation.

The reading never adjusted to the youngest person in the room. It was assumed that if you were present, you were capable. The older children read aloud. Their voices were steady, trained by repetition and confidence. They had learned when to pause, when to emphasize, and when to answer quickly. Their familiarity with the text gave them safety. They belonged in that space. I did not.

I was the youngest in the room. Small enough to be overlooked when tasks were assigned, but never small enough to be excused from responsibility. I sat among bodies that were larger, voices that were louder, expectations that were already formed long before I had arrived. That night, fatigue found me before understanding did. I remember the room clearly. The way the air felt heavy, as if it had been breathed too many times without escape. The way bodies shifted on hard surfaces, restless but obedient. The cadence of sacred language moves forward without concern for who it leaves behind. At some point, my attention slipped. Not deliberately. Not rebelliously. Simply humanly. My eyes grew heavy. The words blurred into sound rather than meaning. I drifted.

When the reading ended, the questions began.

They moved around the room methodically, as stones passed from hand to hand. Each person answered, sometimes confidently, sometimes cautiously, but always with the assurance that they were allowed to speak. Each answer reinforced the order of things. Then the question reached me. I felt it before I heard it. The shift in attention. The pause that signals expectation. The quiet that waits for your voice.

In that moment, fear rose faster than thought. I searched my memory desperately, scanning the fog of half-heard sentences for something solid. Names escaped me. Places blurred.

The sequence dissolved. I could not recall who had done what, or why, or where the lesson was meant to land. I knew nothing except one image. Someone was being beaten.

That was all that had stayed with me. The violence of it. The repetition of the act. The physicality of pain. So when I spoke, that was what I reached for. I used the most dramatic word I knew for it. A word that carried weight I did not yet understand. I said it plainly, without irony, without intention beyond survival. I was not trying to shock. I was trying to prove that I had been there, that I had listened, that I was not absent. The room changed immediately. First, stillness. A collective intake of breath. Faces frozen in a way I had not seen before. Then laughter erupted. Sharp, sudden, surprised. It was not cruel laughter. It was not meant to wound. It was the laughter that comes when something fragile breaks open in a place where it does not belong. The laughter of adults and older children caught off guard by the wrong word in the right setting.

They laughed because it sounded wrong. Because it disrupted the seriousness of the moment. Because a child had spoken too directly about something that was meant to be handled reverently, carefully, with approved language. I stood there, confused, my heart racing. I did not laugh. I did not understand why they were laughing. For me, the image was real. Someone had been beaten. That was not funny. But something important happened at that moment. I was not punished.

My answer, wrong as it was, counted as participation. It proved I had been present. It spared me correction. The laughter, unexpected and uncontrolled, had shifted the room. It softened judgment just enough for me to pass through unharmed. Only later did I learn the details of the story. Who had been beaten. Why had it happened, and how does it fit into the larger lesson. But by then, the moment had already done its work. That night, laughter stood between me and discipline.

I did not understand what had happened in terms of humor or strategy. I did not recognize it as wit, timing, or performance. I only knew that saying something, even the wrong thing, had been safer than saying nothing at all. It was my first lesson in speaking as a survivalist. I did not choose humor that night. I did not practice it or plan it. It arrived uninvited, born from fear and instinct rather than confidence. But it stayed. Looking back, I see that this was the moment humor entered my life, not as decoration, but as protection. A shield discovered accidentally, held awkwardly at first, but effective enough to remember. It taught me that silence could expose you, but sound could redirect danger. That seriousness was not always the safest posture. That sometimes, disruption was not disobedience, but intelligence.

I was seven years old, standing in a room where I did not yet belong, learning for the first time that survival did not always require correctness. Sometimes, it requires courage disguised as a mistake. I did not know then that this instinct would follow me into classrooms, institutions, and adult spaces. I did not know it would become a language I would rely on when authority closed ranks and clarity failed. I only knew that night that I had spoken, that the room had laughed, and that I was still standing when it was over. And that was enough to teach me that silence, in the wrong moment, could cost more than words ever would.

The Weight of Seriousness

As I grew, I learned that seriousness carried status. Girls who were quiet were praised. Girls who laughed too easily were corrected. Laughter, I was taught, suggested carelessness.

It suggested a lack of depth and discipline. Respect belonged to those who spoke rarely and never too loudly. But humor had already rooted itself in me. It surfaced when I was unsure. When I was cornered. When the rules were unclear, and the consequences were not. In primary school, I struggled often. With expectations. With systems that moved faster than my understanding. Humor slipped out of me then, not as performance but as release. A sideways answer. An unexpected observation. Something that softened the moment enough for me to pass through it unscathed. By high school, humor had become visible. And visibility has its price.

It began during class presentations. I was not trying to be amusing. I was trying to organize chaos. If the class needed a plan, I proposed one. If there was confusion, I spoke. Somewhere along the way, usefulness was mistaken for entertainment. People began to look at me differently. They laughed before I spoke. They waited for me to say something light, even when the topic was not. They stopped calling me by my name. Instead, they used the names of characters I played in jokes, versions of me I had not chosen but had inhabited convincingly enough. I became an expectation. When I was quiet, people felt cheated. When I was serious, they were offended. There were days when my insides were heavy with thoughts I did not know how to articulate, and still I was expected to make the room lighter. Humor, once a shield, became a uniform.

In high school, sports were mandatory. Running, drills, discipline. The body is measured by obedience. I did not belong to that language. In my first school, when everyone ran laps, I climbed onto the basketball structure and sat there, legs dangling, watching the others circle the field. When they returned, breathless and confused, they found me still above them. "This is my sport," I said. They laughed. Teachers sighed.

Me in front of the body building area in school

No one made me run. I was not proud. I was relieved. When I changed schools, I hoped for anonymity. A new beginning. This school was co-ed. I told myself I could be serious here if I wanted. I could rest. Sports registration came again. I scanned the options like a strategist. I chose what looked least demanding. When that failed, I registered for bodybuilding. No one told me I could not. Every afternoon, others ran until they were exhausted. I sat with a small weight in my hands, lifting it slowly, deliberately. When questioned, I showed my registration. The rules protected me. I was not breaking them. I was inhabiting them creatively. This was not a rebellion or a confrontation. This was rebellion as adaptation. Humor without laughter. Resistance without shouting.

The Drum and the Uniform

Later, during a period of training that braided history, culture, and military discipline into a single demanding routine, I learned how easily truth could turn into an offense. Mornings were not simply early. They were rigid. We woke to uniforms and commands, to boots that had to be worn correctly, and to silence that was not restful but enforced. Every movement was watched. Every pause meant something. Silence here was not a choice. It was an instruction.

In my Training uniform

By evening, bodies were tired in a way that did not ask permission. People searched for softness wherever it was allowed. Many chose traditional dance, a way to shake off the day, to move without orders. I chose drums. Drums felt safer. They required rhythm, not endurance. Listening, not obedience. I could be present without proving strength.

I was playing when the soldier approached. He watched me for a moment before asking where I was from. It was a simple question, the kind that usually carries no weight. I answered honestly, without preparation, without strategy. He told me I was lying. The accusation startled me, not because it was frightening, but because it made no sense. There was nothing remarkable about my hometown. No prestige attached to its name. If I were inventing a story, I would have chosen somewhere admired, somewhere impressive. I said this plainly, not to challenge him, not to defend myself, but because the truth felt obvious.

That was my mistake. In that system, you do not correct seniors. You do not explain yourself. You do not offer logic when the hierarchy has already decided. Truth does not outrank authority. It never has. By the next morning, the story had taken a different shape. It was no longer about where I was from. It was about disrespect. About questioning. About stepping outside the invisible line that keeps order intact. Punishment was discussed openly, as if my presence were no longer required for the conversation. What struck me most was how quickly my honesty had been translated into defiance.

At some point, someone joked that I should be married off as a discipline. The comment was absurd, exaggerated enough to invite laughter. And laughter came, spreading easily through the group, loosening what had begun to harden. I joined in. "If that means we eat first," I said, "then it is acceptable." The room shifted.

It was subtle, but unmistakable. The tension loosened its grip. Faces softened. The seriousness that had been building lost momentum. Humor, unexpected and unthreatening, changed the direction of the moment. Nothing was resolved formally. No apology was offered. No rule was revised.

But the severity faded. The punishment never arrived the way it had been announced. I learned something important then.

There are environments where protest only sharpens punishment. Where logic is heard as challenge and explanation as rebellion. In those spaces, humor can become a quieter form of resistance. Not loud enough to threaten authority, but strong enough to protect dignity. I did not win that moment. I survived it. And sometimes, survival is its own kind of victory.

As a child, I often left home without permission. I believed cleanliness equaled safety, so I bathed, dressed neatly, and left. Logic, I thought, would protect me. I walked for hours. Met people. Returned with messages meant for my mother. I delivered them honestly. Only afterward did I realize what I had revealed. The room would fall silent. Then laughter. Then the consequences. In school, I once read aloud from a borrowed book. A word had been altered. A crude word. I read it without understanding. The class froze. Eyes turned. Judgment hovered. The teacher checked the book. The alteration was discovered. It was not mine. Laughter followed. Relief followed. I was spared. Even embarrassment, I learned, could be survived if it did not harden into shame.

Humor and Authority

As I grew older, humor began to take on a different posture in my life. It was no longer something I reached for in moments of fear, no longer a shield raised quickly when I felt exposed. It softened. It settled. It began to move outward, not to protect me from the world, but to meet it. During my internship at a radio station, I learned this in a way that stayed with me. Interns existed on the margins of certainty.

We filled gaps, covered absences, and kept things moving when others arrived late. On weekends especially, presenters would ask someone to start their programs, to load playlists, to hold the space until they arrived. I was trusted with that responsibility more than once, and I took it seriously, even when I was unsure.

One Saturday, a senior leader walked in with a musician and asked me to upload a song and play it. There was no discussion, no explanation. The request came with the quiet confidence of authority, and I followed it without question. The song played. It was long. Longer than I had expected. Longer than anyone had prepared for. When the presenter arrived and realized what was happening, his alarm was immediate. He looked at me, genuinely confused, and asked how I could have programmed a song like that for his show. I did not argue. I did not explain the chain of command or defend my decision. I laughed. Not carelessly, but honestly. I told him a story about a musician whose single songs were so long that they were often mistaken for three. The comparison landed gently. He laughed too.

The tension dissolved. The mistake, once sharp with the possibility of blame, became human. Not an error that demanded punishment, but a moment that allowed learning. I was not reduced by it. I was not dismissed. I was trusted again. That was new.

Later, I began to notice something else. People talked to me differently. They lingered after conversations. They shared uncertainties they did not share elsewhere. Not because I was authoritative or impressive, but because I was approachable. Humor had created room. People brought questions they were afraid would sound foolish. Stories they worried might be judged too quickly.

Doubts they carried quietly because they did not know where else to place them. They told me it felt easier. Lighter. As if speaking did not require armor. I realized then that seriousness was not the only path to respect. That authority did not always need to announce itself through firmness or distance. Sometimes it arrived softly, built not on fear, but on trust.

Pain and Shared Laughter

We lost a friend, and with him, we lost the language we thought we understood. There were no instructions for how to mourn him, no shared agreement on what was appropriate or dignified. Grief did not arrive in a single shape. It came unevenly, catching us off guard, refusing to stay contained. We gathered because being alone felt unbearable. Not to be strong, not to be composed, but because silence felt too large to hold by ourselves. When we began to speak, it was tentative at first, as though we were testing the air. Then the stories started to surface. We spoke of moments we had never voiced while he was alive. Small annoyances. Private affections. Regrets that we had waited too long. We said things we had once feared would sound disloyal or unkind. In that space, honesty mattered more than politeness.

At some point, someone laughed. It surprised all of us. The sound felt almost wrong at first, sharp against the weight of loss.

But it did not stop. Another laugh followed, then another, uneven and fragile. Our voices cracked as we laughed, grief pressing against the edges of the sound. The laughter did not erase the pain. It sat beside it. There were tears. Long silences. Hands covering mouths as laughter turned suddenly into sobs. But we did not apologize for it. We let it exist as it came, unpolished and unplanned.

That was when I understood something I had not known before. Laughter does not always mean lightness. Sometimes it is a way the body releases what it cannot carry alone. Sometimes it is how grief breathes when words are not enough. That was the first time I laughed through pain, not to avoid it, not to soften it, but to survive it.

Humor allowed me to move through systems that were not designed for softness. It allowed me to speak without demanding permission. It allowed me to remain human in places that preferred obedience. Seriousness can command respect, but it often creates distance. Humor opens doors. It invites people closer. It makes truth easier to carry.

Today, humor feels quieter. It no longer shields me. It walks beside me. It reminds me that resistance does not always look like defiance. Sometimes it looks like refusing to disappear. Sometimes, laughter is how we stay.

Chapter 9

What I'd Tell My Younger Self (Now That I Listen)

A **Conversation Across Time**

I imagine her sitting quietly at her desk, her legs swinging just above the floor, her school bag heavier than it needs to be. It rests against the wooden side of the bench, swollen with books, folded papers, half-finished notebooks, and the invisible weight of expectations she does not yet have words for. The desk is etched with faint scratches left behind by other children, other stories. The room smells faintly of paper and chalk, the kind of smell that settles into your clothes and stays long after the bell rings. Outside, the day moves on without noticing her thoughts. Voices pass by. Footsteps echo. Somewhere, someone laughs. Time does not pause for her, even though she feels suspended inside it.

She is ten. Or maybe fourteen. Or sixteen. In my memory, she is all of them at once. She sits with her back slightly bent, not from tiredness but from habit, as though she has learned early how to make herself smaller. Her hands rest on the desk, fingers tracing the edge without realizing it, following the grooves as if they might lead her somewhere safer. There is a stillness about her that adults often mistake for obedience. It is not obedience. It is attention. She is always paying attention.

She looks up when she senses me. Not startled. Not alarmed. Just curious, the way children are when they feel something familiar but cannot name it. Her eyes carry questions she does not yet know how to ask. They are not questions about homework or grades or what comes next on the timetable. They are deeper than that, heavier, and strangely quiet. Questions about why some things feel harder for her than for others. Questions about whether it is normal to feel this much, this early. Questions about whether the world has already decided something about her without telling her first. She is not dramatic. She is not loud. She does not demand space. She exists carefully, as though the room itself might object if she takes up too much of it. She watches before she speaks. She listens before she reacts. She has learned that observation is a kind of protection.

From where she sits, she can see the window. Light spills in unevenly, touching the floor in patches. Dust floats through the air, catching the sunlight for a brief moment before disappearing again. She follows it with her eyes, wondering how something can be visible and invisible at the same time. She does not know it yet, but she feels the same way. She is trying to understand where she belongs in a world that has already begun asking her to fit into shapes she did not choose. No one has explained these shapes to her directly. They exist in glances, in tone, in silence. They exist in the way praise is given selectively, in the way certain questions are discouraged, in the way curiosity is welcomed only up to a point. She senses the rules long before she understands them.

Sometimes she wonders if everyone feels this way, or if it is just her. She does not ask. She keeps wondering to herself. There is safety in silence, or at least the illusion of it. I kneel beside her, slow and careful, as if sudden movement might break the moment.

I am careful not to frighten her, not because she is fragile, but because she has learned to be alert. She turns her head slightly, just enough to see me from the corner of her eye. There is recognition there, even though she does not know who I am yet. Recognition without explanation.

I want her to know that she is safe with me. Truly safe. Not the kind of safety that demands compliance, or politeness, or gratitude. The kind that allows her to exhale without checking first. The kind that does not ask her to justify her feelings or shrink her questions. I want her to know that I am not here to correct her. I am not here to tell her what she should already know, or what she should have done differently. I am not here to rush her toward clarity or confidence or certainty. I am not here to ask her to be better, sharper, stronger, quieter, louder, or more anything at all.

I am here to listen. I listen to the things she has not said out loud. To the tension she carries in her shoulders when she thinks no one is watching. To the way her jaw tightens when she is unsure but pretending she understands. To the small, private negotiations she makes with herself every day. If I stay quiet, I will be safe. If I do well, I will be accepted. If I try harder, maybe I will belong.

She does not yet know that these negotiations are exhausting. She thinks they are normal. She thinks this is simply what growing up feels like. She glances back at her notebook, at the neat lines she has drawn across the page. She likes things to be orderly. It gives her a sense of control. She writes carefully, erasing often, wanting the page to look right. Not perfect, just right enough that it will not draw attention. She has already learned how much attention can cost. I sit with her in that quiet effort. I let the silence exist without filling it. She relaxes a little.

Not completely, but enough. Enough to rest her chin in her palm. Enough to let her thoughts wander for a moment.

Her mind drifts. It always does. She imagines herself somewhere else, somewhere wider, somewhere less defined. She does not yet imagine success or recognition or achievement. She imagines space. Room to move. Room to breathe. Room to exist without explanation. She feels these longings more than she understands them. They arrive without words. They sit beside her like unanswered questions. I want to tell her that nothing about this is wrong. That confusion is not failure. That quiet does not mean empty. That sensitivity is not something she needs to grow out of. But I do not interrupt her thoughts. She deserves to have them uninterrupted for once. So I stay beside her. I let her swing her legs. I let the chalk dust settle. I let the day continue outside without demanding her participation for a moment longer. I am not here to change her. I am here to witness her. And in that witnessing, something softens. Not dramatically. Not all at once. Just enough for her to feel, even briefly, that she is not invisible. That someone sees her exactly as she is, without waiting for her to become anything else. She does not look at me again. She does not need to. The room remains the same. The desk is still scratched. The bag is still heavy. The world outside still moves on. But inside, something has shifted. And for now, that is enough.

Who She Was Then

At ten, she was finishing primary school in the Northern province, playful, light, still unaware of how deeply the world could press into a person. At fourteen, she had already learned how to watch carefully, how to be quiet in the right moments, and how to read rooms before speaking. By sixteen, she was living in the Southern province, attending a science school, far from the familiarity of the North that had shaped most of her life. She was, above all, a schoolgirl. Nothing extraordinary on the surface. No dramatic declarations. Just a girl moving from one classroom to another, from one city to another, carrying more inside her than anyone could see. She did not yet know how to name what she felt. She only knew that something was shifting inside her. That she was no longer only playful, but thoughtful. That fear had entered her vocabulary, quietly, without asking permission.

Fear did not arrive all at once. It came in layers. Fear of not being enough. Fear of not belonging anywhere fully. Fear that something about her would not be accepted by the world. There was anger, too, and confusion. A constant desire to escape, sometimes from places, sometimes from situations, sometimes from feelings she did not yet understand. She felt fear most strongly at fifteen and sixteen, when the world began asking harder questions and offering fewer answers. And yet, there was something else growing alongside that fear. Spirituality. At first, it was casual, almost playful. She moved between places of worship easily, simply because she had time, because she was curious, because everyone around her seemed to choose something, and she wanted to understand why. Religion, at that stage, felt like a game the adults were playing. But later, it became a choice. A real one. Not inherited. Not assigned. Chosen. She grew quiet in ways that surprised people who thought they knew her. She meditated. She reflected. She connected with things that felt deeper than the noise around her. People who knew her before did not recognize this version of her. And yet, this version felt truer.

She began to feel connected to a purpose, even though she could not yet explain what that purpose was.

Her dreams were not loud ambitions. They were soft wishes shaped by empathy. She wanted to help people whose hearts felt heavy. People who could not talk about their pain. People who carried things silently. She wanted to be someone who could relieve that weight, not with magic, not with grand gestures, but simply by being present. She wanted to leave a smile behind. On everyone she met. She did not know how that would happen, or if it even could. She only knew that this desire lived inside her, steady and sincere.

Even then, her dream was not about herself. It was about others.

The Insecurities She Did Not Name

Perfectionism followed her quietly, the way a shadow follows without announcing itself. It did not arrive as pressure or ambition, but as a soft, constant awareness of being watched, measured, evaluated. She learned early that doing things well brought approval, and approval felt like safety. So, she tried. Not loudly. Not rebelliously. She tried carefully. She wanted to do things right. Not extraordinary, not impressive, just right enough to avoid correction. Being good became a form of protection. Being acceptable felt like the closest thing to belonging. She paid attention to details others overlooked, corrected herself before anyone else could, and carried an invisible checklist inside her mind. Am I behaving properly? Am I speaking at the right time? Am I taking up too much space?

And beneath all of it lived a quieter question. Am I enough?

Enough to belong somewhere without effort. Enough to be chosen without explanation. Enough to be treated the same way as others, without having to earn it repeatedly. She did not ask these questions out loud. They felt too fragile, too exposing.

Instead, she worked harder. Tried longer. Smiled when unsure. Stayed silent when confused. Friendships confused her in ways she could not articulate. She watched how closeness formed between others, how easily some people slipped into connection, how quickly alliances seemed to shift. She noticed differences that were small but powerful. A choice of words. A tone. A moment missed. Something that seemed insignificant yet changed everything.

She replayed conversations in her head long after they ended. She wondered if she had said too much or too little. If she had misunderstood something, everyone else seemed to grasp instinctively. She searched for a clear mistake, something tangible she could fix. But often there was nothing obvious. No argument. No betrayal. Just distance. And the absence of an explanation hurt more than an answer ever could. She told herself she must be doing something wrong. Even when she could not name it. Even when there was no evidence. The assumption settled quietly inside her, shaping the way she approached people, the way she hesitated before trusting, the way she prepared for rejection before it arrived.

More than anything, she feared being a misfit forever. Not in a dramatic way. Not as someone who stood apart intentionally. But as someone who never quite blended in, no matter how much she tried. Someone is always slightly out of rhythm with the world around her. She reassured herself with time. She was young, after all. Things change when you grow. People change. Places change. She told herself this often, the way one repeats a sentence in the dark to stay calm. But there was a question that lingered beneath those reassurances. Unspoken, persistent, refusing to disappear.

What if this is who she was everywhere she goes? What if the discomfort is not temporary? What if the distance follows? What if belonging is something others stumble into naturally, while she has to keep reaching for it, always just short of grasping it? She did not say this fear out loud. Saying it would make it real. So she carried it instead, folded carefully into her days, tucked between effort and hope. And even as it weighed on her, she continued to show up. Continued to try. Continued to believe, quietly, that somewhere, somehow, there was a place where she would not have to ask these questions at all.

There was the day she carried Sorghum beer and special bread to school, carefully packed into her bag for a friend. Her intentions were simple. Kind. Thoughtful. But when the bag spilled, and the smell filled the classroom, no one asked questions. No one waited for an explanation. She remembers the silence. The eyes. The heat of embarrassment. The internal debate. Should I explain myself? Should I defend myself? In the end, she said nothing. She cleaned the mess. Hide the bag. Covered it with dust so the teacher would not see.

It was not the biggest humiliation she would ever experience. But it was the one that taught her how quickly kindness could be misunderstood, and how lonely it could feel to stand inside a story no one else wanted to hear.

Even then, strength was present. Persistence. Positivity. The ability to love easily. Ambition, though she did not yet know what shape it would take. Focus. Empathy. Self-assurance, even when she doubted herself. She noticed stories. Followed them. Returned to them. She could focus deeply on things she chose, and once she committed, she did not let go easily. Others noticed too.

Teachers who advised her to choose English, even though no one else did. Teachers who recognized her mathematical ability. A headmistress who saw potential she had not yet claimed for herself.

In scouts, they named her vigorous for her endurance. Not because she was loud. Not because she complained. But because she did not cry when tested. Because she endured quietly. At the time, she did not understand why that mattered. She only knew that if she wanted to cry, she would choose when and where.

What I Would Whisper to Her Now

I would sit close and speak softly, not because the words are fragile, but because she has learned to listen more carefully when voices are gentle. I would not rush. I would wait until she feels the quiet settle, until she knows this is not another instruction, not another expectation disguised as care.

You do not have to be perfect. You only have to be real.

I would let the sentence rest between us. Let it land without explanation. She has spent so long trying to be correct, appropriate, acceptable, that the idea of being real might feel unfamiliar. Almost risky. She might not believe me at first. That is alright. Truth sometimes needs time to be trusted.

I would tell her that holding emotions inside her body is not strength. That swallowing fear, anger, sadness, and confusion does not make them disappear. It only teaches the body to carry weight it was never meant to hold alone. I would tell her that strength is not silence. That endurance does not always look like stillness. That feeling deeply is not a flaw to be managed, but a signal to be understood.

I would tell her that loneliness can exist even when people surround you. That it can sit quietly in the middle of conversations, in classrooms full of noise, in rooms where everyone else seems connected. And I would tell her this loneliness does not mean something is wrong with her. It does not mean she is ungrateful, broken, or difficult to love. It simply means she is human, and that her inner world is larger than the space she has been given to express it.

I would tell her that worrying about doing everything right will slowly make her forget how to live. That constant self-monitoring turns life into a performance, not an experience. That there is more to existence than avoiding mistakes. That joy does not arrive only after approval. That mistakes are not evidence of failure, but proof of movement.

I would tell her that the fear she feels in her body is not imagined. That the unease, the vigilance, the awareness of being unsafe at times, of being watched or exposed or vulnerable, is real. That fear of harm, of being harassed, of being crossed without consent, is not weakness or exaggeration. It is knowledge shaped by experience, by instinct, by a world that does not always protect those who are quiet or young or female.

And I would say this clearly, without hesitation. None of it was ever her fault.

Not the fear. Not the caution. Not the moments she froze or stayed silent or second-guessed herself. None of it disqualifies her from dignity or safety. None of it makes her responsible for the harm she was trying to avoid.

Then, without ceremony, I would lift the burden of perfection from her shoulders. Gently. Slowly. Like removing something she has carried for so long that it has shaped the way she stands.

She might feel strange without it at first. Lighter, but uncertain. As if part of her balance is missing.

I would stay with her in that feeling. Let her adjust. Let her learn what it feels like to exist without constantly proving her worth.

And when she is ready, I would remind her that she was never meant to carry all of this alone. Her interest. Her positivity. Her love. Her belief that she could do anything. Her belief that she could love everyone. Those beliefs were innocent. And beautiful. And worth protecting. I think of the day she decided to donate blood at sixteen. She had finally reached the required weight. Fifty-nine kilos. She was proud. Impatient. Afraid it might disappear if she waited. So she lied about her age. She told her friend what to say if she died. She donated anyway. She felt dizzy. She sat down often, convinced that at any moment she might collapse. And yet, she did it. Looking back, I laugh gently. Seriously. At the fear. The courage mixed so tightly together. She did not know then that this pattern would follow her for years. Fear and action walk side by side.

Looking Forward

I would tell her never to forget her values. Her principles. Her virtues. I would tell her that consistency matters. That integrity, kindness, humility, and love will carry her further than approval ever could. And finally, I would tell her this. One day, you will listen to yourself more than the noise around you. One day, you will sit with the woman you are still becoming. And I hope, when that moment comes, she will smile back at you.

The girl stands up now. Lighter than before. She walks back into her life, still uncertain, still learning, but no longer alone. And I remain here, grateful that I finally learned to listen.

CHAPTER 10

The Work Is Not Done, But I Am Enough

A **Quiet Victory, not a Loud One**

I remember sitting with numbers and conversations instead of dreams and panic, and realizing how unfamiliar that felt. For so long, my days had been filled with urgency rather than intention. I was used to thinking in terms of survival rather than structure. Every decision carried weight because it felt like one wrong move could undo everything we were trying to build. But that day was different. I was not calculating how to survive the next few weeks. I was looking ahead. And for the first time, that future did not feel fragile. Stability had always felt like a word meant for other people. Something distant, abstract, almost theoretical. I could imagine it, but I could not touch it. It was something I quietly hoped for, without trusting it too much. That day, I realized stability was no longer just an idea. It was something we were shaping slowly, deliberately, with our hands. It was present in spreadsheets, in planning meetings, in conversations that no longer began with apologies.

We were budgeting ahead instead of asking for more time. That alone felt revolutionary. For years, money conversations had been heavy with embarrassment and tension. I was constantly negotiating delays, promising that things would get better soon, hoping people believed me.

I hated those moments. Not because people were unkind, but because I felt like I was always asking them to carry the uncertainty with me. That burden never sat well in my heart. Now, I could project. I could say, "This is what we can afford," and trust the answer. We were paying people on time. That mattered more to me than any external recognition. Paying people on time meant respect. It meant dignity. It meant that the work they were doing was no longer held hostage by chaos. It meant that we were no longer operating from desperation but from responsibility.

I could see how the system was beginning to hold itself together. Not perfectly, not effortlessly, but honestly. The girls we worked with were no longer only stories of urgency and need. They were becoming part of a structure that could support them consistently. We were no longer reacting to crises alone. We were building something that could prevent them. Before that shift, everything had felt like survival. Every conversation came with an apology, even when I did not say the words out loud. I apologized with my tone, with my hesitation, with the way I softened requests that should have been clear. Every delay felt personal, as if it reflected my character rather than circumstances. Every promise carried anxiety because I was never fully sure I could keep it. I lived in a constant state of alertness. My mind was always scanning for the next problem, the next gap, the next thing that could fall apart. There was no space for calm reflection because everything felt urgent. Even moments of progress were brief. I celebrated quietly, cautiously, afraid that joy might invite disappointment.

In 2022, something shifted. For the first time, I could say, "This is what we can do next year," and mean it. Not as a hopeful guess, not as a motivational sentence, but as a grounded plan. I could sit with the people I worked with and speak honestly about what was possible.

That honesty felt like relief. I did not have to oversell or undersell our reality. I could simply describe it.

What surprised me most was how the process itself began to change. It became kinder. Meetings were no longer charged with fear. Conversations had room for questions instead of blame. Decisions were made with clarity rather than urgency. There was more listening and less scrambling. More intention and less reaction. I began to notice how much energy survival had been consuming. How much of myself had I been holding back just to keep things moving? Stability did not make the work easier, but it made it healthier. It allowed us to think about people, not just outcomes. About sustainability, not just speed.

And somewhere in all of this, something inside me softened. The work was not done. I knew that deeply. There were still challenges ahead, still gaps to fill, still systems to strengthen. But something inside me was no longer scrambling to prove its worth. I was no longer chasing validation through exhaustion. I was no longer measuring myself solely by how much I could endure. I felt content. And that feeling was unfamiliar enough to make me pause and examine it closely. Contentment did not arrive with fireworks. It arrived quietly, in moments of calm acknowledgment. In the realization that I did not need to explain myself constantly. In the knowledge that the work had roots now. In the confidence that even when things went wrong, we had the capacity to respond. Contentment did not mean complacency. It did not mean I stopped caring or striving. It meant I was no longer at war with myself. I could appreciate how far we had come without dismissing how far we still had to go. That was new for me. For most of my life, progress had never felt enough. I was always looking ahead, always measuring, always preparing for the next hurdle.

Pausing felt dangerous, as if stopping to acknowledge stability might make it disappear. But that year taught me something important. Stability grows stronger when it is recognized. Peace deepens when it is allowed to exist. I learned that it is possible to be ambitious without being anxious. It is possible to build something meaningful without constantly sacrificing yourself. That contentment does not dull your purpose; it grounds it. That realization did not mark an ending. It marked the beginning of a different kind. A beginning rooted not in panic, but in presence. Not in fear, but in trust. And once I felt that, even briefly, I knew I could never go back to surviving alone.

When Ordinary Moments Become Sacred

Peace did not arrive as rest. It arrived as gratitude. There are moments now that still surprise me with their gentleness. I walk into rooms I once dreamed of being invited into, not because I applied or chased, but because someone thought of me and called. Rooms filled with business leaders, decision makers, people who belong there so naturally that they forget how extraordinary it can feel to arrive. Sometimes I sit there quietly, aware that I am lucky. I do not know how others experience those rooms, but for me, they still carry a sense of disbelief. And yet, as meaningful as those moments are, they are not what move me the most.

What stays with me longer are the messages. The insights. The voices of people who used something we created and found value in it without being asked. When feedback comes from outside our systems, from people who owe us nothing, it feels different. When someone tells us that something we built helped them, or answered a question they did not even know how to ask, it lands deeper. There was a moment when I saw a satisfaction score reach ninety-nine percent. I remember thinking, almost shyly, that I wanted to save it, to keep it close, to remind myself on harder days that love had been felt on the other side of our work. Even when the feedback is familiar, even when it is repeated, it still touches me. Because it is never just data. It is proof that care travels, and that what we build with intention leaves traces beyond us.

How Success Changed Its Meaning

Now, success feels quieter and more demanding at the same time. It no longer announces itself loudly or waits at the end of a visible finish line. It shows up in moments that require honesty rather than celebration, restraint rather than momentum. This version of success asks more of me than the one I used to chase, because it demands awareness and courage even when there is no applause. I have learned that success is knowing when something is not working and having the strength to stop. Not stopping because I have failed or run out of ideas, but stopping because I respect my energy enough to protect it. There was a time when I believed pushing through was the only proof of commitment. I equated exhaustion with dedication and persistence with virtue. Walking away felt like weakness.

But I have seen what happens when effort continues without reflection. Energy drains quietly, creativity dulls, and resentment builds beneath the surface. Success, I realized, is recognizing failure early enough to learn from it instead of glorifying burnout. It is choosing to pause before the damage becomes irreversible. It is refusing to confuse endurance with wisdom. Stopping, I learned, can be an act of care. Reflection is not retreat. It is an invitation to listen. When I step back, I am not abandoning the work. I am giving it the attention it deserves.

Reframing is not quitting. It is a willingness to ask better questions, to reshape direction instead of clinging to plans that no longer fit.

This shift was uncomfortable at first. There is a strange vulnerability in admitting that something is not working, especially when you have invested time, hope, and identity into it. But there is also relief. Relief in honesty. Relief in choosing alignment over momentum. Relief in allowing myself to adapt rather than force outcomes that no longer serve the purpose I began with. Success now lives in the space between awareness and decision. In noticing the subtle signs that something has reached its limit. In listening to discomfort instead of silencing it. In trusting myself enough to make adjustments without needing external permission. It is less about arriving somewhere and more about staying present with where I am. Less about chasing a future version of myself and more about honoring the one who exists today. I no longer measure success by how far I push, but by how truthfully I respond. By how responsibly I manage my energy. By how willing I am to change course when clarity demands it. This understanding has softened my relationship with work and with myself. I no longer feel compelled to prove my worth through constant motion. I am learning that success does not require me to disappear into effort. It asks me to stay awake, attentive, and honest. And in that awareness, I find a deeper sense of accomplishment. One that does not rush me forward, but allows me to stand still long enough to choose wisely.

When I Stopped Trying to Prove Myself

There was a time when proving myself cost me more than it ever gave me. I did not realize it immediately. At first, it felt necessary. I believed that if I explained myself well enough, worked harder, or adjusted my tone and pace, I would eventually be understood. I thought belonging was something I had to earn through effort. In 2018, I paused. Not in a dramatic way, and not by stepping away from everything, but with intention. I began to observe where my energy was going. I noticed how often I was trying to fit into worlds that were not designed with me in mind. Worlds with unspoken rules, familiar faces, shared references, and expectations that did not include someone like me. Even when I showed up prepared, committed, and capable, I often felt like I was still standing at the edge.

I tried harder for a long time. I adjusted myself in small ways, hoping it would make the space more comfortable for others. I explained my choices, my background, my work, my vision. And yet, no matter how much effort I put in, the sense of belonging never fully arrived. That was when I began to see the cost. It took three times more energy for me to prove myself than it did for those who naturally matched those spaces. The exhaustion was not just physical. It was emotional. It was quiet and cumulative. What troubled me most was not the rejection, but what it was doing to my inner world. My peace was being disturbed. I was spending so much time trying to be understood that I was losing touch with why I was doing the work in the first place. The constant effort to justify my presence was pulling me away from what mattered. It was turning meaningful work into performance.

That realization was painful, but it was also clarifying. I understood that the energy I was pouring into validation was energy I could not recover. And more importantly, it was energy that deserved better use. I could invest it in building something real. In strengthening the work itself. In protecting my focus, my health, and my sense of self. That year, I made a quiet decision. I stopped explaining my existence.

I stopped shrinking or reshaping myself to make others more comfortable. I did not become less committed or less ambitious. I became more selective. I learned to conserve my strength instead of offering it up for approval. This shift did not happen overnight. There were moments when the old instinct returned, when I felt the urge to justify myself again. But each time, I remembered the cost. And each time, I chose differently. 2018 became a turning point, not because everything changed externally, but because something settled internally. I learned that not every space requires my explanation. Some require my absence. And that choosing where to place my energy is not avoidance. It is respect.

That was the year I stopped proving myself. And in doing so, I finally began to protect the work and the person behind it.

What helped me arrive here was not certainty. It was exposure. Meeting people from different communities, cultures, and countries showed me that I was not alone. Had I stayed only within the world I grew up in, I might have believed that I was the problem. But stepping into other spaces helped me see that there were many ways to live, lead, and belong. I learned. And then I unlearned. Many of the rules I had accepted without question no longer applied. I realized that some of the things I had spent years worrying about were never essential to begin with. Mindfulness became part of this learning. Not as something religious or symbolic, but as a daily practice of checking in with myself. While traveling. While resting. While pausing. Simply asking, "How am I right now?" That question changed everything.

I do not dream of legacy in titles or numbers. I think of light. I believe everyone carries light inside them. Not the same shape. Not the same intensity. But something that can be used.

And what matters is how we choose to use it. Light can illuminate. Or it can burn. If there is one thing I hope people remember, it is that they carry their own light and that they choose to use it for something good.

Some of the moments that moved me most were never planned. Girls receiving pads or jobs matter deeply to me, but those were intentional efforts. The moments that surprise me are the ones that reach back across time. People from primary school. From high school. People I barely remember. They find me on social media and remind me of something I said or did when I was nine. When I was ten. When I was too young to understand that kindness leaves footprints. They tell me how something small gave them hope. And I sit there wondering how I even afforded to do those things. How I found the courage. How I did not know I was doing anything at all. Those messages remind me that impact often begins before intention. And that we shape lives without realizing it.

I still make mistakes. Recently, after weeks of travel, exams, and unexpected opportunities, exhaustion caught up with me. I overslept before an important interview. Missed it entirely. The hotel staff panicked. People called. Messages flooded in. I woke up confused, disoriented, and certain that I had ruined everything. And yet, somehow, the interview still happened. And somehow, I still won. I laugh about it now. Not because it was easy, but because it reminds me that perfection was never the requirement.

I am still becoming. I want to complete my MBA. I want to get married. I want to visit the last continent on my list. Australia is still waiting. I want to pause without guilt. To move forward without panic. There are still things ahead of me. And that no longer scares me.

Becoming, for me, is connecting the dots. It is finding clarity in exhaustion when the work has meaning. I feel grateful when my name becomes associated with impact rather than noise. It is hearing my name and knowing it stands for something that matters, even if I did not plan it that way.

I enjoy that now.

For Anyone Who Feels Behind

You do not have to arrive at the same time. I wish someone had told me that earlier, and not as a slogan, but as permission. For a long time, I measured myself against other people's timelines, their speed, their milestones. I believed that arriving later meant failing, that taking longer meant lacking something essential. It took years to understand that timing is not a measure of worth. You just have to arrive. That is all.

Some paths are longer because they carry more learning. Some journeys take time because they are asking you to grow in ways that are not visible yet. Progress does not always look like movement. Sometimes it looks like endurance. Sometimes it looks like waiting, recalibrating, gathering strength in silence. Trust the process, even when it feels uneven. Trust it when you cannot explain it to others. Keep going, not because you are certain, but because stopping would mean abandoning yourself. You are allowed to pause. You are allowed to rest. You are allowed to breathe and adjust your pace.

But do not stop. There is a quiet kind of courage in continuing without rushing. In choosing persistence over comparison. In believing that your arrival, whenever it happens, will still matter. And it will.

I thank my younger self for daring to start. For returning after rejection. For not giving up when it would have been easier to disappear.

And to my future self, I make this promise. I will pause when I need to. But I will not stop. The work is not done. But I am enough.

CHAPTER 11

Across Borders

The first time I traveled alone for work, I carried more than a suitcase. I carried my culture, my assumptions, my fears, and a version of myself that had never been tested outside familiar ground. Until then, travel meant family visits to neighboring countries. It meant going somewhere with people who knew me, who spoke like me, who moved through the world the way I did. But professional travel was different. It demanded something else. It demanded that I stand on my own.

In 2015, I traveled to Kenya for the first time in a professional capacity. At that point, I had only one culture inside me. I carried it confidently, unaware of how deeply it shaped me. Kenya confronted me with difference, not in a dramatic way, but in a subtle and transformative one.

I was there primarily for leadership learning. Professionally, it was enriching. But culturally, it was awakening. I noticed something immediately. People expressed themselves openly. They spoke about how they felt without hesitation. In my culture, we were more reserved. We held things in. We filtered emotions carefully before letting them out. Watching people in Kenya say what they felt, directly and naturally, unsettled me at first. Then it inspired me.

I remember thinking, "Why are we so reserved? Why do we block how we feel?" There was a lightness in the way they moved through life. It was easier for them to say what they thought. It made relationships clearer. It made misunderstandings shorter. It made authenticity possible.

From Kenya, I learned the power of expression. Not speaking carelessly, but speaking honestly. Finding a way to say what you think without aggression, but also without fear. That lesson stayed with me. I have now visited Kenya more than twenty times. Each visit deepened that learning. It was not just a country I visited. It became a mirror in which I saw parts of myself that needed freedom.

In front of CISCO

In 2016, I traveled to the United States for the first time. Unlike Kenya, I went there without expectations. I did not imagine what it would be like. I did not compare it to anything.

That trip was powerful in a different way. We met high-level women leaders in major technology companies. We visited Facebook, Google, Visa, and Cisco. Coming from an IT background and having completed Cisco certifications, stepping into Cisco as a visitor was surreal. At my age, sitting across from women leaders at these companies, asking questions, sharing worries, and realizing they shared similar doubts changed something inside me.

Until then, I had unconsciously believed that people at that level lived in another world. That their struggles were different.

That their confidence was permanent. Listening to them speak about challenges and insecurities bridged that imagined gap. They were human.

They had worries. They had faced uncertainty.

It made ambition feel realistic.

We visited Texas and California. California felt different, busy, and fast. My impression of the United States at that time was shaped by that busyness. I remember thinking, people here do not have time. Even sharing a drink requires scheduling. I felt like there were people everywhere, yet something about connection felt scarce.

When I returned home, I told myself I could visit, but I could not live there long term. I felt they lacked what I call people. The unstructured presence. The time to just be.

In 2017, I traveled to Uganda and Ethiopia. Uganda felt familiar, like neighbors. I was there for digital security learning. What stayed with me most was a lesson about boundaries. In one of the sessions, I observed something subtle. People respected each other's boundaries without needing to fully understand them.

Where I grew up, if something did not make logical sense to you, you felt justified in dismissing it. But in that room, I learned that respect does not require agreement. If someone says, "This is my boundary," I do not have to understand why before respecting it. If they choose to explain, that is their choice. But respect comes first.

That shifted how I relate to people.

Ethiopia was different again. I went there to learn about natural dyeing and textile coloring. Technically, it was enriching. Culturally, it was layered. The program was sponsored by the United Nations, and during our stay, there were planned protests in the city.

One day, we were told not to leave the hotel because protests would happen near our training venue.

I was confused. How do you know there will be protests? If something wrong is going to happen, why not stop it before it begins?

At the time, I did not understand the complexity behind such situations. I only felt that it was unfair. Were they protecting some people and not others? Did everyone know? That experience exposed me to the reality that systems operate differently from what we assume.

Despite that tension, I loved Ethiopia's cotton. Their textile knowledge. Their protection of culture. I learned about their calendar and how their year is counted differently from ours. It confused me, but it also humbled me. There are many ways to measure time.

In 2018, I traveled to India for four months. It was my first time there, and it stretched me deeply.

During my time in Bangalore

I was based in Bangalore, but we traveled to different cities. The program was international. Only seven of us in the class were Indian. Each of us had a local buddy. My Indian buddy made daily life easier. Living in a hostel with many girls from different backgrounds expanded my understanding of diversity.

What struck me first was open-mindedness. People understood things beyond their fields. Someone in medicine could discuss politics. Someone in engineering could debate philosophy. I kept asking myself, how do they know so much? Why did they not stay confined to one area?

It challenged my idea of specialization.

India was loud. Coming from a quieter environment, I initially felt overwhelmed. People told me it was normal. Slowly, I adjusted.

When I returned home, the quiet felt strange. I realized adaptation changes you.

Food was another lesson. I believed I could eat anywhere. I was wrong. I do not eat spicy food. I would ask for non-spicy meals, and still receive food with chili. They would say it is not spicy. I would struggle.

Eventually, the hostel staff began washing my portion of food after cooking to remove the spice. For four months, I ate washed food. It sounds humorous now, but it taught me something practical. Before traveling, research food. Prepare. Carry snacks if necessary.

During that period, I visited textile industries. I was still selling clothing then, and I wanted to understand production systems. Observing how textiles were manufactured expanded my entrepreneurial vision.

I also began exploring materials for reusable sanitary pads. In my home context, reusable pads were associated with poverty. People referred me to those who could not afford disposable ones. In India, I met women who chose to use reusable pads. Environmental awareness. Comfort. Preference. It was not about money.

That difference mattered deeply.

They gave me detailed feedback about brands, materials, staining, absorption, and comfort. Even years later, some classmates still send me feedback when they try new brands. It transformed how I thought about product development. I could not build something based on assumptions. I needed user insight.

When I inquired about specific materials, many suppliers said they sourced from China. That answer repeated everywhere. If I wanted certain materials, I had to go to China.

China became a goal.

Before going, I tried contacting Chinese textile factories through email and Google. No response. No calls returned. It felt impossible.

Then I joined a program through Alibaba Business School. When we arrived, they provided local accounts and local phone numbers. The moment I called using a local number, suppliers answered. Not only that, they offered to pick me up from the station and show me their facilities.

For five months, I had struggled to reach them. One local number changed everything.

2019, China; at the Alibaba Business School

That experience reshaped my approach to networking. If someone does not respond, it may not mean rejection. It may mean the wrong channel. Cultural context matters. Sometimes, in-person engagement is essential.

Since 2019, I have consistently sourced materials from China. That one connection simplified years of struggle.

After China, I returned to India for a leadership program in Delhi. Delhi felt different from Bangalore. But more than the city, the program gave me space for reflection.

Before going to China, I had attended a similar leadership program in Kenya. That was a period without intense pressure, and I had to recover. After India, I had lost weight. I had dropped eight kilograms.

My sister used to say I was underweight. When I returned, I joked that she would think I was dying. So, I chose a program where I would not study heavily, not pay rent, and not worry about complex reporting. I wanted to eat, sleep, and regain strength.

For a month, I did exactly that. Eat and sleep. I became known as the person who always announces the tea and lunch breaks. I gained five kilograms. I proudly told my sister I was now 54 kilograms. She responded that I should be 62. I decided I was done trying.

Those programs taught me something subtle. When I am not stressed, I am kinder, more present, and more attentive to others. In that Kenya program, many people remember me as the one who had time for them. The nice one. It made me reflect. Everyone can be kind when they are not overwhelmed. Stress changes how we appear to the world.

During these travels, my work on sanitary pads continued. In Ethiopia, I evaluated cotton materials but found them unsuitable. In India, I explored banana fiber textiles in Hyderabad, though it was complex. Everywhere, I searched for materials aligned with functionality and sustainability.

Later, I returned to the United States for another fellowship. This time, my experience shifted dramatically. I was placed in Iowa. Iowa felt different from my previous U.S. visits. It felt like home in certain ways. Farming landscapes. People with time to talk. Families hosting us to share culture.

It balanced my earlier perception of the U.S. as too busy. In Iowa, people were present.

We visited neighboring states. I visited a zoo in Omaha for the first time. Coming from a place where animals roam freely, seeing them enclosed felt strange. I questioned why they were confined.

It was a new lens on conservation and control.

At the end of the fellowship, we attended a summit in Washington DC. In Iowa, we were twenty-five fellows. In DC, there were about seven hundred.

I am not naturally inclined toward large networking events. I prefer fewer, deeper connections. While some people collected a hundred contacts, I focused on meeting those I could genuinely connect with.

Even if I did not maximize energy in that space, relationships formed there later translated into real collaboration. Some fellows visited my company. Some came with their families. The impact of being part of the Mandela Washington Fellowship alumni network grew over time.

With the Invest2Impact award

Around that period, I received two major awards. First, in October 2019, from UNDP, worth 5,000 dollars. Then, in November of the same year, I received another award from Invest2Impact, worth 25,000 dollars.

It was my first time receiving such recognition. We traveled to Uganda in December to connect with other UNDP Award winners.

Global exposure did not just give me stamps on a passport. It reshaped my internal architecture.

Kenya taught me authenticity. The first U.S. visit taught me that leaders are human. Uganda taught me respect for boundaries. Ethiopia taught me cultural complexity. India taught me open-mindedness, adaptation, and user-centered design. China taught me strategic networking. Iowa taught me that perceptions can change. Large summits taught me to honor my limits.

Across all these journeys, I learned something consistent. Travel is not about movement. It is about expansion.

Expansion of thought. Expansion of empathy. Expansion of possibilities.

Each country added a layer to my leadership. Not by making me louder, but by making me more aware. Aware that culture shapes communication. Systems shape access, and context shapes opportunity.

And perhaps most importantly, I learned that growth requires exposure.

You cannot solve problems in isolation forever. At some point, you must see how others approach similar challenges.

You must observe what works elsewhere. You must accept that your way is not the only way.

Looking back, I see how these global experiences intertwined with my personal impact. They refined my product. Strengthened my networks. Challenged my assumptions. And most of all, they changed how I see myself in the world.

I am no longer just someone from one place trying to prove something. I am someone shaped by many places, carrying lessons from each, building something that reflects all of them.

Global exposure did not erase my roots. It deepened them.

It gave me the confidence to speak across cultures. To negotiate across systems. To learn without defensiveness. To adapt without losing myself.

And in that process, it expanded not only my network, but my sense of what is possible.

CHAPTER 12

The Power of Networks

In the earliest days of my company, there were no investors waiting. There were no venture capital meetings, no polished pitch decks, no due diligence processes. There were only convictions and whatever money I could gather.

The company was self-funded at first. It was my savings. It was my sister's support. It was family stepping in, not because they fully understood what I was building, but because they trusted me enough to let me try. The first year, it was mainly my sister and me. There was no external capital. No institutional backing. Just belief stretched across limited resources.

Looking back, that beginning shaped how I approach capital even today. When you start with your own money, every decision carries weight. Every mistake feels personal. Every success feels earned.

But as the company grew, I knew that if we were to scale, self-funding would not be enough.

The biggest challenge in raising my first round of capital was trust. Not just trust in the business model, but trust in me. Investors were not only asking, can this business work? They were asking, can she do this?

At the same time, the nature of my business complicated things. It was impact-focused. Social.

Not purely profit-driven. Some investors prioritize financial returns. Others prioritize impact. Navigating those two expectations at once required clarity that I did not fully have at the beginning.

Before I had a strong network, convincing people to believe in my vision felt like trying to push a door that did not know it was meant to open. I did not have anyone established who could vouch for me. No one who could say, I know her. She will deliver.

So I went through the programs.

First internships. Then incubators. Later accelerators. Each program became a credibility layer. The people managing these programs observed my work. They saw my consistency. They saw that I did what I promised. That mattered.

Referrals from program managers became the bridge I did not have in the beginning. If they trusted me enough to recommend me to their peers, that was my first form of endorsement. I learned very quickly that reputation compounds.

Networking was not natural to me at first. The first networking event I attended did not feel comfortable. I could see people effortlessly talking to dozens of others. That was not me.

So, I made a rule for myself. At every event, I would speak to three people. Just three. Intentionally.

I would leave each of them with my card. That was 2014.

One of those three people later wrote me an email recommending me for a program in Kenya in 2015. She believed I should attend. I did not even know what grants were at that time. I had to Google the term. I was coming from a business background, not from the world of programs and fellowships.

When she nominated me, people around me discouraged me.

They were unfamiliar with the idea that someone would pay for your flight ticket and give you money to attend a program. The program was in Kenya, and it was shortly after a terrorist attack there. So, there were fears about safety and legitimacy.

But I chose to trust her.

That decision changed my trajectory.

The program in Kenya was an eye-opener. It was structured intentionally to build relationships across cohorts. Previous fellows graduated when we joined, so we could connect with them. When we graduated, the next cohort joined. The network did not end at the program. It continued on shared platforms. Recommendations flowed naturally.

It was the first time I saw how being part of a network could unlock opportunities without constant pitching. If someone was part of that fellowship, there was an assumption of vision and courage. That made introductions easier.

That was the first moment I realized relationships were not optional. They were infrastructure.

The second defining moment came in 2019 at a social impact summit in Kenya, where Ashoka was present. Since 2015, I have wanted to become an Ashoka Fellow. It was not a program you applied for. You are nominated. At that summit, I was very clear with myself. I need someone in this network to nominate me.

We were preparing presentations when someone pointed out that the East Africa director of Ashoka was approaching. My entire group whispered that this was my moment. I spoke to him. We took a picture.

He gave me his card and told me to remind him about the nomination form. It was a long form. Very detailed.

In the end, I did not become a Fellow at that time. But something more powerful happened. He recommended me to more than four programs, including funding opportunities far larger than the fellowship I initially wanted. That was when I understood something critical. A connection does not always give you what you ask for. Sometimes it gives you something better. The third defining moment happened in 2024 at a conference in Mexico. It was described as an unconference. There was no rigid agenda. People joined sessions as they wished. Many attendees were investors or representatives of investment organizations.

I attended as a social entrepreneur seeking fundraising opportunities.

2025, Abu Dhabi; at the Goalkeepers event by the Gates Foundation

But the first lesson investors shared with us was unexpected. Build relationships before fundraising. They spoke openly about frustration. At work, everyone looked at them as money machines. No one connected with them as people. They wanted conferences to feel human, not transactional. Hearing that shifted something in me. Until then, much of my fundraising had been formal. Check eligibility. Submit proposal. Follow up. At this conference, I saw the emotional dimension of capital. Investors are human. They carry fatigue. Expectations. Pressure from their own funders.

If I approach them only with a pitch, I may miss the opportunity to connect.

So I began changing my strategy. Instead of leading with the proposal, I led with conversation. Understanding who they are. What they care about. Whether our missions align.

Sometimes those conversations did not immediately lead to funding. But when we met again at the next conference, the relationship was warmer. The proposal had context.

And in some cases, by aiming for a smaller amount at first, I discovered there was a larger possibility available, simply because we had built trust.

Trust is currency before capital becomes currency.

A defining funding breakthrough also came in 2019 from a connection that challenged me on systems change. In one evaluation, I scored highly on mission and entrepreneurial spirit. But I struggled to articulate how my work influenced systems change.

Instead of rejecting me, that connection recommended me to a program focused specifically on systems thinking. It shifted my mindset from linear impact to systemic influence.

After completing that program and adjusting how we worked, that same connection later recommended us for significant funding in 2023 and 2024. It was the biggest funding we had received up to that point.

Sometimes what feels like critique is preparation.

Building trust before we had a proven track record required accountability. If I promised something, I delivered. If funding was restricted, I followed the guidelines.

If it were unrestricted, I still would have asked about expectations.

If circumstances changed on the ground, I communicated.

Investors often require participation beyond the funding period. Reporting. Events. Introductions. Sometimes it feels exhausting. But I remember how they showed up when I needed them. So I show up when they need me.

Interestingly, many of our most successful fundraising rounds came through previous investors recommending us to new ones. They had already done due diligence. Their endorsement unlocked trust before we even entered the room. Authenticity reduced misunderstandings. If I were not transparent at the beginning, frustration would emerge during implementation. Projects become real when they are executed. Misalignment surfaces quickly.

Investor hesitation often centered around traction. Who else has invested? What progress have you made?

Early investors who believed in the entrepreneur, not just the numbers, helped unlock bigger investments. Once one trusted name appeared on our portfolio, others felt safer.

I also learned to work with partners of larger investors first. If I was not yet ready to access a major investor directly, collaborating with their trusted partners created familiarity. When those partners recommended us, doors opened faster.

Cultural intelligence became increasingly important.

Between 2014 and 2020, much of my network leaned toward American foundations and corporations. My proposal style aligned well with their expectations and with their creativity, ambition, and innovation.

In 2021, I intentionally studied European funding culture. It was different. Due diligence was deeper. Slower. They often preferred working through European organizations on the ground. Some even visited in person.

At the Obama Foundation office

At first, I wondered whether they did not trust local people. But over time, I understood that this was their system. Once you deliver on promises, communication within that ecosystem travels fast. If you fail to deliver, that communication also travels fast.

Currently, a significant portion of our funding comes from Europe.

International exposure absolutely expanded access to capital markets. But it also refined the strategy. Before 2024, my approach was eligibility-focused. If I did not meet the criteria, I did not apply. I calculated the probability. I prioritized opportunities where we had a higher chance of success.

After 2024, I added a human dimension. Sometimes rejection is not about the proposal. It is about timing. Emotional readiness. Relational depth. Once initial funding came in, maintaining long-term relationships required consistent communication. Not just transactional reports. Impact updates. Growth stories. Annual impact reports shared with former funders.

They want to see what their support helped grow.

Mentors, peers, and fellow entrepreneurs have been powerful contributors to our fundraising success.

At the Clinton Global Initiative Annual Meeting

The first fellowship in 2015 alone opened access to platforms that ultimately translated into more than 350,000 dollars in cumulative funding.

Peer entrepreneurs became unexpected funding sources. Through shared platforms and mutual recommendations, we raised more than 400,000 dollars through peer referrals.

Local programs managing European funding streams also played a role. Working closely with them allowed them to observe our work firsthand. Their recommendations led to more than 500,000 dollars in funding.

Funders often connect us to CEOs of companies we once considered competitors. Those conversations are eye-opening. Different countries. Different economies. Yet similar challenges. Shared lessons.

A valuable network shares mission alignment. If values do not match, implementation becomes painful. During COVID-19, some investors suggested pivoting into entirely different sectors for profit. We resisted. If funding pulls you away from your mission, the cost is too high.

The right network reduces wasted time and emotional strain.

Balancing genuine relationships with business objectives increases success rates. When you are genuine, you increase the probability of achieving project outcomes. That credibility leads to repeat funding and high-level referrals.

Beyond capital, networking expanded my leadership. It taught me to see the human side of investors. To dream bigger.

At the White House

It is difficult to dream beyond what you see. Growing up in a rural area, I once thought owning a small boutique was the highest aspiration. Exposure to global entrepreneurs and investors expanded my imagination.

Now, I approach fundraising with a long-term vision. Not one transaction, but sustained collaboration.

Networking did not just help me raise capital. It helped me grow into someone capable of managing it responsibly.

Conclusion

There is a particular kind of stillness that arrives not when everything is finished, but when enough has been understood. It does not feel like a celebration. It feels like clarity. Not the sharp kind that answers every question, but the softer kind that allows you to stop fighting the unknown quite so hard. This is where I am now. Not at the end of a journey, and not at the beginning either. Somewhere in the middle, where reflection becomes possible. Where the noise of proving begins to fade, and the work of becoming settles into something more honest. Where I can look back without urgency and forward without panic.

For a long time, I believed that courage would feel louder when it arrived. That strength would announce itself clearly, perhaps with confidence, perhaps with certainty. I believed that one day I would wake up without doubt, without fear, without the quiet questions that once followed me everywhere. That day never came. What came instead was something less dramatic and far more useful. I learned how to stay. I learned how to remain present in my own life, even when answers were incomplete. I learned how to continue without needing reassurance at every step. I learned how to accept that growth does not eliminate uncertainty; it changes your relationship with it. The fear did not disappear. But it no longer had the final word.

Looking back, I can see how many moments I once misunderstood as weakness. Hesitation. Exhaustion. Doubt. The need to pause. The urge to step back before stepping forward again. I used to believe these were signs that I was not strong enough, not ready enough, not built for this kind of path. Now I understand something different. There were signs that I was paying attention. Strength, I have learned, is not the absence of fear. It is the ability to remain intact while carrying it. It is the decision to keep choosing yourself even when the world has not yet agreed with your direction. It is the quiet discipline of continuing to show up, long after the excitement has faded and before results become visible. There were many moments when stopping would have been reasonable. Moments when the resistance felt too heavy, when doubt felt practical rather than emotional, when stepping away could easily be justified. I did not keep going because I felt powerful in those moments. I kept going because stopping felt like abandoning something important inside me. Something younger. Something hopeful. Something that had waited too long to be heard.

If there is one truth this journey has taught me, it is this. Becoming does not happen in leaps. It happens in repetition. In return. In choosing again what you once chose with fear. Resilience is rarely visible from the outside. It looks ordinary. It looks quiet. It looks like persistence on days no one applauds. This book is not a record of victories. It is a record of endurance. Along the way, I have learned that being the first often means being alone for longer than you expected. That path without maps requires patience that cannot be rushed. That support does not always arrive when you need it most, and when it does arrive, it often comes quietly, disguised as one person, one moment, one small sign that you are not entirely unseen.

I have also learned that not everyone will understand your choices. Some will doubt them. Some will question them. Some will only support you once your effort looks safe, once your risk has been converted into results. This is not cruelty. It is fear wearing familiar faces. People protect what they know. The unfamiliar unsettles them. Do not mistake that discomfort for a verdict on your worth. If you have ever felt tired of explaining yourself, tired of justifying your curiosity, tired of carrying hope without witnesses, I want you to know that exhaustion is not failure. It is evidence that you have been trying something real. You are allowed to rest without giving up. You are allowed to pause without abandoning your calling. You are allowed to take care of yourself without losing momentum.

The work does not require you to break yourself to be meaningful. There is a version of strength the world celebrates loudly. It is sharp. It is impressive. It moves fast. There is another version that receives far less attention. It is slower. It is quieter. It builds foundations instead of headlines. This book belongs to that second kind. I have come to understand that leadership, in any form, does not begin with influence. It begins with responsibility. With learning how to protect what matters before asking it to grow. Building safety before demanding courage. With understanding that resilience without care is simply endurance in disguise. Somewhere along this journey, without announcing itself, that shift happened for me. I stopped measuring progress by how much I could tolerate, and started measuring it by how well I could sustain myself. I stopped glorifying struggle and began respecting steadiness. I stopped postponing myself in the name of responsibility and began allowing myself the same care I had always extended to others.

This was not a moment of revelation. It was a series of small decisions made quietly. Decisions to prepare before leaping. To ask for help without shame. To say no without apology. To trust that protection is not a reward for suffering, but a condition for living well. I have become, in many ways, the woman I once needed. Not the one who promises everything will be easy, but the one who ensures things are as safe as they can be. The one who understands that dignity lives in systems, not speeches. The one who knows that real care is practical, not performative. If there is a younger version of you somewhere inside, still waiting for permission, still wondering whether they are allowed to want what they want, I hope this book has spoken to them gently. I hope it has reminded them that worthiness is not earned through struggle. It is inherent. That they do not need to finish everything today. That growth does not require visibility to be real.

You are already becoming, even when it feels slow. This is not the end of my work, and it is not the end of yours. Becoming does not conclude neatly. It continues. It adjusts. It deepens. There will be more doubts ahead, more decisions that feel heavy, more moments when the path ahead is unclear. That does not mean you are lost. It means you are alive inside your own choices. If these pages have done anything at all, I hope they have offered you permission. Not permission to be fearless, but permission to be honest. To move quietly if needed. To take up space when you are ready. To trust that your story matters even before it becomes visible. You do not need to make a loud noise to move forward. You only need to move honestly. One breath. One decision. One quiet act of courage at a time. This book was never meant to be about one life. It is a mirror for many. If you saw yourself reflected here, then the story has already served its purpose.

About the Author

Blandine Umuziranenge is a Rwandan social entrepreneur, innovator, and Founder & CEO of Kosmotive, a pioneering women's health enterprise transforming menstrual, maternal, and reproductive care across Africa. Her path, shaped by early hardship and an unyielding pursuit of education, spans IT, Filmmaking, Social Innovation Management, Leadership, and more than 70 global fellowships, including the Miller Center for Global Impact Accelerator, the Obama Leaders Program, the Mandela Washington Fellowship, and the Clinton Global Initiative (CGI).

Practical, hands-on, and empathetic, Blandine learned to move between strategy and detail: pitching ideas one day, fixing systems the next, and always listening to the people she served. Kosmotive began as a small effort to meet clear needs in her community and grew into a platform that blends purpose with real-world solutions. Under her guidance, the venture focused on dignity, inclusion, and creating jobs and skills where there were few.

In 2025, Blandine's work gained global visibility: she became a Top 20 finalist in Africa's Business Heroes, won the FemSTEM Africa

Award, was featured on the Nasdaq billboard in Times Square, was recognized among ABCD Media's 100 Most Impactful Voices, and was selected for develoPP Ventures Cohort 8. She also represented Rwanda and Africa at global stages, including Goalkeepers in Abu Dhabi and Commitment to Action at the CGI Annual Meetings in New York, where she advocated for menstrual justice and women's health equity.

Through Kosmotive, Blandine has expanded her impact across multiple African countries, merging sustainable product innovation with digital health solutions, flexible payment systems for menstrual equity, and job creation for women. Her leadership is rooted in empathy, resilience, and the belief that communities can rebuild with dignity when given the tools and opportunity.

Blandine's story is one of resilience, vision, and purpose, building Kosmotive not just as a company, but as a movement for health equity. Through her work, she continues to champion girls' and women's rights, inspire emerging leaders, and reimagine what African-driven innovation can achieve.

This book brings forward her journey - from trauma to transformation, from local challenges to continental solutions - and offers honest, practical lessons on leadership, purpose, and the power of building something meaningful from scratch.

www.ingramcontent.com/pod-product-compliance
Lightning Source LLC
Chambersburg PA
CBHW022052050726

47591CB00002B/502